BLACK SHEEP
WHITE COP

Savannah EXPOsed

2nd Edition

Kevin J. Grogan

Jacque and Vivian,
Thanks for the
support. Enjoy the
ride.

[signature]
EXPO

Dedication

This book is dedicated to the men in the arena-- the Al Catos, the Ray Cheveriers, the Rob Santoros and the Alan Sammons of law enforcement-- the guys from whom you will never hear excuses like "Not my job" or "That's all I can do."

This book is for the guys who, at the cost of their home, health and well-being, do not know the meaning of the word "quit" because law enforcement means that much to them.

This book is my thank you to the men and women with whom I have served and have always credited with any success I have achieved. I learned something new and valuable every day from being surrounded by consummate professionals. I thank them for showing me how The Game is played and for their patience with my errors.

In the pages that follow the reader will encounter unsung heroes in the thin blue line growing thinner. Remember them before they are all gone.

"It is not the critic who counts, not the man who points out how the strong man stumbles or where the doer of deeds could have done them better. The credit belongs to the man who is actually in the arena, whose face is marred by dust and sweat and blood, who strives valiantly, who errs, who comes up short again and again, because there is no effort without error and shortcoming; but who does actually strive to do the deeds; who knows great enthusiasms, the great devotions; who spends himself in a worthy cause; who at the best knows in the end the triumph of high achievement, and who at the worst, if he fails, at least fails while daring greatly, so that his place shall never be with those cold and timid souls who neither know victory nor defeat."

Theodore Roosevelt

Table of Contents

Foreword

Savannah, Georgia, in the year 2017 is a city in turmoil.

The violent crime rate continues to spiral out of control and has reached the point where residents no longer feel safe in the historic houses lining quaint streets that attracted them to the Hostess City in the first place. Savannah is a city at war with itself and paralyzed by a widening racial divide that no mayor black or white has been able to heal. The city currently has a population that is 62% minority majority, more than half of whom live at or below the poverty level. For all the improvements in the downtown business district in the past few years there are people living a few short blocks away in the same squalor for generations. Odd how the Savannah of today has the same feel that it had when I joined the Savannah Chatham Metropolitan Police Department at the end of 2004: the second largest urban historic district in the United States surrounded by a sea of despair.

Millions of tourists are attracted to Savannah each and every year to walk our cobbled streets and meander through the squares and gaze at the architecture. Jones Street, the loveliest lane in the entire district, is home to multi-million-dollar four-story townhouses with retail establishments on the ground floor and lavish residences and inns above. Some of the wealthiest people in the world own second and third homes here and while walking the 2-square-mile historic district it is easy to get lost in the beauty of the Spanish moss hanging from live oak trees. It is also easy to walk just far enough to change the scenery entirely: drift too far east and the tourist finds less touristy spots, like the 500 block of

Waldburg and Park. Drift north and walk straight into Fred Wessels Housing Project. Heading west can be equally hazardous, ending up in Frazier Homes or Kayton Homes or on Montgomery and Lorch streets, none of which are highlighted on the map of tourist attractions. It is not uncommon to find tourists parking their vehicles in the heart of the projects which to look at seem like reasonably friendly places until one notices the posted warnings: *No Trespassing, Residents Only* and *Drug Check Point.* Around the next corner the tourist is more apt to discover the boarded up windows of a crack house than a house museum. These two widely divergent worlds intersect and interact thousands of times daily in Savannah, both legally and illegally.

The police departments of Chatham County and City of Savannah merged in 2005. None of us on staff knew how long the transition would last at SCMPD or how smoothly it would run. The City Department was largely black, the County mostly white. County Corporals were considered to be Supervisors; City Corporals were not. The County had better pay and benefits, and conflict was created when co-workers compared pay slips to discover that City employees were being paid after five years what County employees were paid to start. County Mounties had take-home rides; City cops walked home.

Chief Dan Flynn presided over the new law enforcement entity and Chatham County Chief Robert Oliver became his deputy. Suddenly, the future became more uncertain for officers who thought promotions would not come as fast as before or not at all. And all of it combined to create a rather hostile work environment that went off like a time bomb ten years later, destroying the department.

To complicate matters further, Chief Flynn announced that he would retire at the end of 2005, ushering in Willie Lovett as Savannah's first black police chief. The shift in racial balance was like an earthquake, especially when a black mayor was already at the top of local government. But of all the differences created by the SCMPD merger and changes in command, the biggest conflict arose over Savannah's city council taking the reins of the police department and forcing the Chatham County Commission to take a back seat. Both governing bodies were to have equal say, but Savannah was always squeezing the county for greater financial input while pushing their priorities further down the list.

Twelve years later, the situation has not improved at SCMPD headquarters or city hall. City and county governments have reached an impasse on law enforcement. Communication has broken down to the point where Savannah mayors and Chatham County Commission chairmen refuse to talk about SCMPD unless the media compels it. To date, mayor and chairman have been unable to fix anything related to law enforcement. Thus, the department sits neglected by a mayor who does not know what to do and a chairman who knows what to do yet does not want to do it. Pity the poor Savannahian who flees the city for the safer suburbs only to discover that they are paying for services that they do not receive.

The attrition rate among officers at SCMPD that had always been high was made worse in the wake of the scandal that sent Chief Lovett to prison in 2015. The following year was the first in nearly twenty years that the department was fully staffed. But even with a full contingency of 605 sworn officers, Savannah is still 200 shy of recommended strength, and ten percent are always in some sort of training phase in a department where the few remaining veterans are looking for the exits and are not compelled to train newcomers. Worse, it is the stated objective of too many recruits that their plan is to let SCMPD train them and then find a better job elsewhere with departments hiring only experienced officers. Savannah in the process has become the farm team for other jurisdictions and at Savannah taxpayer expense.

Savannah racked up 53 homicides in 2015 and another 50 murders in 2016, 20 of which remain open cases, representing a shocking spike of 65 percent over the prior seven years. Aggravated assaults likewise skyrocketed over 50 percent for the same time period. No doubt these figures directly attributed to the defeat of a popular incumbent mayor in 2015 but the rate of violent crime remained unchanged for the first year of the new administration with no sign of abatement. Claims that crime is in decline is a smokescreen for the fact that the number of arrests is in decline and the reason for this charade is to hide from the public the fact that police are not allowed to do their job around here anymore.

Through it all the single question that I am asked most often by friends and concerned citizens is:

Why doesn't SCMPD bring back the Expanded Patrol Operation that slashed crime rates by 15 percent in 2006?

The answer is not easy, isn't pretty, and is the subject of this book.

Introduction

When I was a kid I thought a book would be written about me someday. I dreamed I was going to be a famous boxer or hockey player. Maybe a comic book instead of a novel, but I knew I was destined for stardom. But by the time I had logged twenty years of combined service in the United States Army and law enforcement, I had encountered subjects better than me that books should be written about, and that is how I ended up writing this one.

My law enforcement career came to a screeching halt on the side of a highway, the perpetrator of a DUI in a company car that spelled automatic termination from the Savannah Chatham Metropolitan Police Department (SCMPD). Enough newspaper articles about my plight and subsequent prosecution for DUI and false statements were generated to fill a book that I did not want written. And while strategizing on how I was going to get back into The Game, I came across a guy who was running for mayor of Savannah in 2015 and had written a blog in which he cited my case as an example of just how bad the situation had become at SCMPD. Not that he was critical of me, far from it. He had taken up my defense, publicly posing the all-important question:

How can the District Attorney prosecute a detective for false statements at the same time he is repeatedly called to testify in the same court on behalf of the prosecution in other criminal cases?

It was a very good question and one that deserved a good answer, an answer that was not forthcoming. But still the candidate continued to ask it. At a time when my circle of support had dwindled down to a few, the loudest voice with the largest audience in Savannah took up my cause.

While offering his own solutions on how to fix SCMPD, which was in the throes of the scandal that sent the chief to prison and caused one-third of the department to resign, the candidate asked for public input in coming up with ways to fix problems that the current administration refused to address and had admittedly ignored for years. And I thought: I can tell this guy what is really going on with SCMPD and hoped that if he was serious that he might actually do something about it.

At our initial meeting I made the candidate aware of things that he did not know about SCMPD. Turns out the candidate is a successful author, among other things. He is also-- and I mean this as the highest compliment-- NOT a successful politician. When I finished laying out the broad strokes of the rise and fall of SCMPD, the candidate suggested that I write it all down. Even if I did not publish a book, he said, just getting these things off my chest would be therapeutic while waiting on my day in court, now dragging into the second year of Purgatory.

So I sat down to write the book I always thought I would be the subject of but it started out much differently than my childhood fantasy. I tore into everyone who ever wronged me and I complained about a system designed to fail. Then suddenly it hit me like a pugil stick, something my Sergeant Major said to my unit during my first week at my first unit in the Army:

You don't like it? Ask yourself what are you doing to make it better?

11

His admonition reminded me that I have always sought to be a part of the solution, not the problem, and the memory of what Command Sergeant Major Barrett said changed the entire direction of this book. I stopped dwelling on all of the perceived wrongs and concentrated on the concrete positives I have witnessed and how I have an opportunity here to shed light on a small band of amazing individuals who, if I were not to write about them, the public might never know about.

I concentrated on the Expanded Patrol Operation, the last successful pro-active policing initiative by SCMPD that reduced violent crime in Savannah by 15 percent, and the high point in my career in law enforcement. I thought about the guys I served with, some of whom-- like me-- came to a less than flattering finish to their career and whom, if you Google their name, you might consider them to be criminal. So at the same time I have this chance to tell you about the good in this garden of evil, I also take this opportunity to show, as in every story, there are two or more sides. Please be advised, however, that I will also address those pillars of this community whose actions might make you think otherwise of their standing.

Lastly, I will take this chance to weigh in on what is happening in America and the disturbing trend of viewing the police as the bad guys. Real heroes in blue uniforms with badges do exist and I am going to introduce you to some of them. Even though these shining examples come from a tiny town like Savannah, the ideal holds true nationwide.

In the end, I have written the book I always thought I would be the subject of but not the hero. Stories of good and evil, but not so much about me. This is, more importantly, a book about my brothers in arms and my heartfelt admiration for their uncompromising dedication to duty.

Ultimately, this book is about standing up for what is right and accepting responsibility for wrongs, having erred and come up short, but still striving to do good deeds.

Kevin Grogan

Chapter One
Savannah gets EXPOsed

If there is one thing Savannah hates, it's a dead white girl.

On New Year's Day 2006, a 19-year-old student at Mercer University named Jennifer Ross became the first homicide victim of the year after succumbing to a gunshot wound sustained during an armed robbery on Christmas Eve 2005. She had been dancing with her daddy at a cotillion only a few hours before and was walking with friends through Orleans Square at 3 a.m. when they were accosted by three black men demanding money. Ross bucked the jack, she refused to give up her purse, and was shot in the back attempting to flee. The publicity that this crime received was unprecedented in Savannah media. Dubbed the "Debutante Murder," the death of Jennifer Ross spurred an outrage that highlighted a racial and economic divide that residents knew only too well and feared that visitors would be surprised to learn.

The murder of Jennifer Ross created a clash between city hall and Savannah's business elite. Bankers, real estate brokers and owners of stores bearing their family name camped at the Chamber of Commerce and from behind its massive granite columns fired accusations at the gold dome across the street that our mayor was not doing enough to combat crime. Dr. Otis Johnson-- only the second black man to serve as mayor-- caught hell for "black crime," which really meant that Savannah's white upper crust was pissed that a black man had the audacity to shoot a white girl, and they demanded to know what the black mayor was going to do about it. Before Mayor Johnson could respond, a new anti-crime citizens group called Save Our Savannah held public hearings where white residents raised more hell and demanded that the city build walls around public housing to keep the criminals inside and put video cameras on every lamppost to track them when they got out.

We don't care if crack addicts shoot each other, said a Save Our Savannah spokesman. *All it's going to take is for one tourist to be murdered downtown and that's it for Savannah!*

Mayor Johnson's measured response was understandable: the racist attacks on city hall must stop so that an effective strategy to stop all crime could be adopted. He asked that those mourning the loss of Ross move past the emotional part of the discussion and toward a more rational discourse, noting that we weren't there yet. Worse, the Mayor feared we were teetering on the brink of going in the wrong direction: Murders on the poor side of town were of little concern to the average citizen. When a black person gets killed it makes the news but when a white person gets killed, special committees are formed to look into the problem.

Crime in Savannah is more of an issue when a white person dies, Johnson noted, then bolstered his defense by reminding his constituents that he had made curbing crime a priority since taking office two years prior by holding town hall meetings poorly attended, accused other black leaders of apathy, and issued a task force report criticizing police for setting low crime-fighting goals for officers who spent too much time sitting behind a desk instead of hitting the streets.

Mayor Johnson looked his detractors dead in the eye and pointed out that for the past two years he had not heard from a single member of

15

Save Our Savannah about crime until the Ross slaying, painfully pointing out that they were too intelligent to be clueless but apparently had more important things to do at the time, like count their money.

Now it has come home to roost in their backyard, said Mayor Johnson, evoking the specter of Malcolm X, and further stoking the firestorm over the public recognition that our quaint little tourist trap was racially divided.

More than 1,000 mourners packed St. John's Episcopal Church and spilled out onto the sidewalks for the funeral of Jennifer Ross. An intrepid reporter from the *Atlanta Journal-Constitution* pointed out what no reporter from the *Savannah Morning News* would dare remark: that the wealthy, mostly white mourners were there to make a political statement as much as grieve the dead. Eight months prior to the Ross murder, a black 27-year-old mother of three was fatally shot in the head by a stray bullet while chatting with friends on the corner of West 38th and Harden streets. There was a vigil with about 100 people and a makeshift memorial of homemade signs and teddy bears erected on the spot where she died but other than that, there was little fanfare or demand that her killer be brought to justice.

No one who mourned the loss of Jennifer Ross gave a shit about Shante Cooper. Including anyone from the *Atlanta Journal-Constitution*.

Enter Willie Lovett.

Willie Lovett had been a Major in the Savannah Police Department since 1998 and was already 32 years into his service to the city, having received the rare 30-year Medal for Distinguished Service, when he made it known that he was interested in becoming Chief. When the SPD merged with the Chatham County Police Department to become SCMPD, the man he would later replace, Dan Flynn, appointed Lovett as the assistant chief of police. Less than a year later, with the public in an uproar over black crime, Chief Flynn retired and at the end of December 2005, Willie Lovett was appointed interim chief of police by city hall. That his promotion came at the exact same time Jennifer Ross was gunned down and on the heels of a blistering task force evaluation was the brutal twinned twist of fate leading to the formation of the most effective crime suppression unit the city has ever seen.

Lovett had been near the top of command structure going on eight years but this was his first shot at being top dawg. The exceptional thing about him was that Willie Lovett was Savannah born, Savannah bred and, when he dies, he'll be Savannah dead. This was not just another position for him. This was his home. After serving in the United States Army and a tour of Vietnam, he returned to Savannah where he had served ever since. He had ideas on how to police the town and how the department should be run and now he had an opportunity to do things his way. And for the benefit of Save Our Savannah, the interim chief wanted them to know that his first initiative would be an aggressive patrol of the public housing projects bordering the historic district.

It is one thing to become interim chief and another thing to be the first black police chief, and quite another to take command during a racially charged crisis. To complicate matters further, the department was plagued by 50 vacancies in a 580-officer force. Savannah police were among the worst paid law enforcement officers in the nation, in a town with a murder rate second only to Atlanta and twice that of rival Charleston. Affluent white Savannahians who were afraid that a black police chief presiding over a black police department would not go to war against a black criminal element beat a path to predominantly white surrounding towns like Pooler and Richmond Hill, where they continued to throw around their considerable weight in running the town they had abandoned when they weren't running their mouths about rampant crime statistics. If Lovett was to earn his permanent rank as chief, he was going to have to take control of the embattled city from the first day of his interim command and bring down the full weight and force of his department on the sons and grandsons of friends and neighbors he had known all his life.

Some of Savannah did not think he would do it.

Responding to the heat deflected by a defensive city hall generated by Savannah's piping hot business community, Chief Lovett looked to a trusted friend, Sergeant Greg Capers, and told him that as interim chief he was determined to police all of Savannah-- not just the 'hood and the hysterical district-- in that same way our first black mayor Floyd Adams had promised to be accessible to everyone-- white and black, rich and poor-- and to that end he asked Capers to put together a unit of highly aggressive officers to add muscle to the patrol division, known as the Expanded Patrol Operation (EXPO). Lovett knew Capers was not afraid to make decisions. But Capers surprised his mentor when he decided against taking the assignment.

Capers had worked special ops before while serving under Chief David Gellatly, who ran a close-knit para-military style department wherein everybody had a job to do and everybody got along. The atmosphere of SPD under Chief Gellatly suited Greg Capers just fine, having recently separated from the United States Marine Corps in 1991.

18

But Capers wanted nothing to do with this new Unit because he knew he'd end up with the worst guys from each precinct, the ones who could be spared. He had seen special units come and go and fail to excel because of bureaucracy and politics.

Commanders are not going to give up their best guys for this new assignment, Capers told Lovett, and there will be too many people trying to influence its direction. And as far as he was concerned, Greg Capers was happy to remain right where he was with the West Chatham Precinct.

Hoping to change his mind, Lovett promised Capers that he would have open-door access to his office and could handpick his own guys.

Any guys?

Any guys, Lovett replied.

Capers stared at Lovett in disbelief. Such a move would send shock waves through Command and create animosity among his Captains but this was a chance for Lovett to make his mark and he was determined to do so. Capers, however, remained skeptical. Before agreeing to take the assignment, Capers told Lovett he wanted to talk to his boys and get their thoughts and input on the Expanded Patrol Operation.

His first calls were to sergeants in different precincts like Sergeant H. Lindsey Rowse, who had an accurate assessment of his personnel but had no political agenda. Capers told Rowse that Lovett intended to circumvent all that crap in order to avoid the pitfalls of limitation and insure that the best men were chosen for the mission. Rowse was as surprised as Capers that an interim chief would stick his neck out like this and under these extraordinary circumstances.

You gotta hand it to Lovett, Rowse said to Capers. *This takes guts.*

His next calls were placed to Sergeant Armando Tamargo and Sergeant Cedric Phillips, these guys knew who the aggressive and best officers were in their precincts and they turned over the names they thought would fit in a unit like EXPO.

After agreeing with his fellow sergeants thus far, they got down to brass tacks: Capers was warned about the toxic political atmosphere in this dirty little town and that he had to be sensitive as to the racial makeup of EXPO. They came up with a list of 17 candidates-- the best of the best-- and Capers delivered it to Lovett thinking there was no way he was going to get all of his top picks, giving him an easy way out of the assignment once denied.

Capers knew that department policy for specialized units generally stated that officers have at least two years experience with SCMPD and that they go through a formal application and selection process. Most of the guys he wanted met those requirements but some, like me, didn't.....he asked for us anyway.

Okay, Lovett said to Capers. *You got 'em.*

All of them?

20

All of them, said Lovett.

Sergeant Capers was stunned when Chief Lovett made it happen. Lovett hardly glanced at the names on the list, as if he expected to find them there. He was not disappointed in the ability of his sergeant to judge character and ability.

Captains were mad as hell to find their precincts robbed of their best talent. Their reaction was on the same seismic level had Major League Baseball informed team managers that their all-stars would not be returning to their team after the break but would remain with the all-star team. It was an arthritic knee-jerk reaction to the fear that by robbing precinct to pay politic every captain would find their crime stats crunched and come up lacking after having lost their best talent. It was left to Lovett to point out to his captains that would not be the case, should EXPO succeed in reducing crime in ways that the present structure did not accomplish. Stats, in fact, would show a reduction in violent crime across the board, benefitting everyone. And then the truth of the matter came into sharper focus: captains could no longer claim credit for crime busting if Capers' Caped Crusaders were crushing it.

Some captains said that the candidates had been picked wrong.

Some captains said that EXPO was just a bunch of renegades.

Some captains went so far as to suggest that the formation of the special unit was illegal and if this was any indication of how Willie Lovett was going to run this department, he was not going to be sitting in the big chair for long. At the same time Lovett was already getting urgent requests from other captains for help in their precincts and to that end assigned Captain Hank Wiley, Commander of West Chatham Precinct, to oversee EXPO and keep the contentious captains off of Greg Capers.

The crime stats are through the roof, Lovett told his command staff, *and that is unacceptable. EXPO is how we are going to take back the city.*

Greg Capers felt a whole lot better about his final decision to take responsibility for EXPO when Wiley was named his direct Supervisor. In the opinion of Sergeant Capers, Captain Wiley was a policeman's police, for there are commanders who want cops to ride their calls and then there are commanders that want cops to go out and do their job. Captain Wiley was one of the commanders who not only encouraged his guys to be proactive in doing police work, he was not afraid to ride with them. If his guys made a mistake in the line of duty, Wiley stood behind them. If the job was done well, Wiley was quick to commend them. If Captain Wiley had his back, Greg Capers figured he had the room to move EXPO in whatever direction Chief Lovett wanted to take it.

*   *   *   *   *

At the same time Chief Lovett and Sergeant Capers were assembling EXPO, I was assigned to the Downtown Precinct as beat officer for Beat 4, consisting primarily of Hitch Village and Fred Wessels Public Housing Projects. I worked B-Watch, alternating monthly from days to nights. It was hell on my nervous system but I liked my schedule because I was exposed to the different tempos of day shift with its higher volume of calls and night shift, which allows more time to be proactive. The worst part about alternating shifts is the effect it had on my body. Spending a month waking up in the morning and sleeping all night to sleeping during the day and working all night is not an easy transition. By the time I adjusted to one shift, I changed back to the other.

Midnights were also tough for a pro-active cop like me who generated a large number of cases because I was called into court to testify for the district attorney the following day. Sometimes I got little or no sleep while on night shift because most of my days were spent in court. The more effective I became as an officer, the more time I spent testifying and the worst part came at the end of every other month when I changed from days to nights and had to double back: I got off day shift at 4 p.m.-- if all went smoothly-- and had to be back at 11:30 p.m. for roll call that night.

That's the way it was and I dealt with it. Nothing kept me from hitting the streets. It is what I lived for. Double backs were tough. It was always hard to stay awake but as luck would have it, those always seemed to be the nights when shit jumped off; same applied to days when I was hung over from the night before.

I worked under Sergeant Andre Coates, a quiet guy that had worked patrol his entire career, and Sergeant Armando Tamargo, who was an extremely aggressive headhunter in Homicide and the Chatham County Counter Narcotics Team (CNT). In 2006, he was midway through a 16-year career with SCMPD that saw him rise from Patrol to Supervisor, to the CNT Major Case Unit, to Tactical Reaction and Prevention, to Robbery, and Homicide.

Tamargo was the ball of fire that pushed me to my creative limits in fighting crime when I wasn't responding to radio calls. I learned a lot

23

from him, not only from watching how he worked but also listening to his explanations about what I was doing well and what needed improvement.

I felt lucky to be part of B-Watch if for no other reason than its cast of characters. There were mellow guys who simply rode their calls and there were pro-active guys who jumped corners, and then there were guys who were a little of both, laid back and aggressive in equal turns. I did most of my training with B-Watch so I knew the guys and they knew me.

Among the most memorable members of my watch was Robie Walp, my first training officer. He earned the nickname "National Security" because he had the misfortune of being a dead ringer for a goofy character in a Martin Lawrence movie and had a hysterical way of communicating with suspects. I remember Walp introducing himself to a gang of thugs saying, *I know you think I'm a redneck but really, I'm from Ohio.*

Walp had been a soldier, military police, and a veteran of Operation Desert Storm and Operation Iraqi Freedom so we hit if off right away. Walp taught me everything there is to know about working the projects. He was a pro-active cop and knew everyone on his beat. I could swear he had the Public Housing Ban List memorized. He was known by everyone in Yamacraw Village in general and the criminal element in particular. All the bad guys knew and respected Walp, and I would not have had the majority of my successes in law enforcement were it not for the time I spent riding with him. A lot of trainees, including myself, tried to rush out of patrol before mastering the art of working a beat. Walp taught me the importance of mastering the beat.

Then there was Corey Cotton, whom I dubbed "Frozone" due to his uncanny resemblance to a character in the popular animated film, *The Incredibles*. Corey was the smooth talker riding Beat 2. I was fresh out of the army and rather naïve when it came to the streets. Corey taught me how to listen to suspects and witnesses and how to pick it apart for the truth. He had a built-in bullshit detector and knew all the telltale signs and pantomimes of the liar. His street interview style was epic and I imitated him word for word until I developed my own game so to speak.

Buck Elliott was another one of my training officers and the beat officer in Hitch Village. He was an intense guy whose claim to fame was having been personal pilot to General Barry McCaffrey during Operation Desert Storm. Buck and Nathaniel Kirkland III-- "Nate the Great"-- rode adjacent beats. Nate patrolled the Ben Van Clark neighborhood, which was filled with a colorful cast of criminal characters and Nate knew them all. Nothing got past Nate and he had the memory of a racetrack bookie when it came to personal scores and accounts. To this day, Nate the Great is by far the most thorough cop I have ever worked with.

Scott McCormick and "Uncle Mike" Embry were two of the more laid back guys who taught me how to keep the big picture in perspective. They taught me that even though I would find violations that there were alternatives to putting people in jail. Police officers have a great deal of discretion and these guys reminded me that the power to deprive a citizen of their liberty is an awesome responsibility. They taught me that just because I had the power to lock up somebody that it did not necessarily mean that I always should. This is a lesson I learned early and learned well: for every misdemeanor I excused, the misdemeanant usually rewarded me at some future point by providing tips on cases I worked as an Investigator and Homicide Detective.

25

B-Watch had a hell of a supporting cast of other memorable characters, including Brian "The Governor" Carelock, Matt "Mr. Incredible" Lake, Kevin "The Goon" McKoon, and John "Captain Caveman" Nevin, all of whom were great to work with.

My partner was Josh Hunt, also known as J-Hunt, who came from Central Precinct in a move Tamargo pulled off while trying to assemble his own all-star team. Josh was a smooth kid and had a magnetic personality. Everybody liked him. But the trait I admired most was that he was what we like to call Natural Police, a hell of a cop in every regard. We hit it off immediately: he was a huge fan of stirring shit and I was a shit-stirrer from the get-go. We quickly made reputations for ourselves in the Precinct and on the street. We also might have been the two middleweights raising hell on the barstools of Sorry Charlie's in City Market and McDonough's on Drayton after midnight shift; I cannot confirm. But it was our work on the streets of Savannah that received the kind of attention that inspired the call from Sergeant Capers I shall never forget:

Son, I'm putting together a crew of ass kickers, Capers said to me. *We're going to go out and put asses in jail. You interested?*

Hell yes, I said.

We are not going to be chasing little old ladies, he continued. *We are going after the worst offenders. We are going to jump corners and clear them of the thugs who are killing off the neighborhoods. I'm going to let you get as creative as you can be in finding ways to get these jokers. But it all comes down to going on the offensive instead of being a reactionary force.*

26

Nothing he could have said could have pleased me more. As soon as the call ended I called Sergeant Tamargo,

This is a chance for you to show what you're all about, Tamargo told me. *All eyes will be watching this one. I think you're cut out for it.*

Thank you, sir, I said.

Just remember: you're a rookie and don't know shit, he said.

Yessir, I said. *copy that.*

Don't fuck this up and make me look like an asshole, he said, by way of congratulations.

Noted, and off we went.

Chapter Two
Start Me Up

I have wanted to be the police for as long as I can remember.

As a kid playing cops and robbers I always picked the good guys, and as soon as I graduated from Westfield State College in 1998, I immediately signed on and went to the police academy two weeks later. My first attempt at field training was thwarted by the college party mode I seemed to be stuck in and a foreshadowing of ominous things to come. The department decided that I should grow up before they let me loose on the mean streets with a gun and a badge. I am Irish by birth, a fighter by nature and so it should follow that I love to drink. I searched my soul and decided that I really did want to be the police, then opted for the United States Army Military Police Corps so that I could get as much related training as possible and also give me a chance to broaden my horizons. I was 23 years old and, with the exception of a few trips here and there, had never been out of New England.

I went to Basic Training at Ft. Leonard Wood, Missouri, and got orders to Heidelberg, Germany, the greatest duty station ever. After arriving at the 529th Military Police Company, the Honor Guard for the United States Army Europe (USAREUR), I immediately deployed to Kosovo in support of the peacekeeping mission.

My next assignment was to the Protective Service Platoon that was responsible for the physical security of USAREUR Headquarters and the personal security of the Commanding General, Deputy Commanding General and the Chief of Staff. Possibly the best assignment a soldier could ask for. I got to see all of Europe and I was around the greatest minds the Army has to offer.

I was shipped off to Sadr City, Baghdad, by way of Fort Stewart, and was assigned to the 549th Military Police Company, 3rd Military Police Battalion, 3rd Infantry Division. We patrolled Sadr City and trained the upstart Iraqi Police, such as it was, and got their stations up and running. It was, to date, the most memorable year of my young life.

I returned from Baghdad in 2004 and transitioned out of the Army. I took a position with the Department of Defense Police at Fort Stewart where the tempo was a little slow. I thought I had a good shot at getting on with the Savannah Police Department. The recruiting office for SPD and the Chatham County Police Department had combined and I joined the last of thecounty hires and was appointed class sergeant. After winning the High Firearms Award, I had a choice of assignments and picked the Downtown Precinct, home to Savannah's nightlife and where I had heard there was a lot of action. Hell, at that point I didn't know shit, so what the hell. Turned out to be a good move for me.

Hitch Village was crazy aggressive and I was its perfect match. Before moving on to EXPO I knew everybody in Hitch Village and Fred Wessels Project, which had become known as East and West Groganistan.

I talked to anyone who would talk to me. If there was a subject I wanted to talk to that did not want to talk to me, I would find any legal way to engage them and if that opportunity did not present itself, I made mental note and waited until I had a justifiable reason for stopping them and getting them to talk. I was fortunate to work with officers who were of a similar mindset and we benefitted from the contacts we made and shared. A cop can never know too much about who is on their beat or what they are doing. When something happens, or more importantly if something is about to happen, we already know who belongs and who does not. That is how law enforcement keeps the public safe and which I learned by watching the best, Walp and Cotton, work their beats.

The general idea behind crime suppression units is to bulk up patrol responses to Part 1 crimes, including murder, aggravated assault, armed robbery and rape. CSU did not get tied down by dispatch calls; they were pro-active patrols that hit hot spots and responded when something big went down, like a shooting or robbery or bar fight.

The design of EXPO was similar to CSU but we were to specifically address high-crime areas that harbored known offenders. The biggest difference between CSU and EXPO was that we were countywide. We went everywhere and responded to any situation that Sarge directed. Even though there is a gratuitous open-air narcotics trade permeating Savannah, EXPO was not designed to work street level drugs. But over the course of our existence we excelled in this area. Sergeant Capers assigned two-man units to provide an automatic back up to anything EXPO encountered and when all units were in the same area, that was a lot of back up.

EXPO's method of operation and mission meant that we would be working alongside the K-9 Unit. It was rare that a shift began without one or two K-9 handlers. Sergeant Greg Ernst, a real cop who always went the extra mile to put bad guys in jail, led the Metro K-9 Unit. Ernie was a no-nonsense, straight-talking leader. He did not mince words when telling me what I did not want to hear but let it be known that he was always on my side. Ernie had been one of the original members of the K-9 Unit when Chief Flynn came to Savannah from Miami-Dade police in 2000. Our K-9 Unit was based on the Miami model and to that end Flynn tasked Sergeant A.J. Haysman and Corporal Ernst with putting together Metro K-9 after studying other K-9 schools, policies and training methods.

The SCMPD K-9 Unit trained at Beck's Canine Service in Wilmington, NC. The breed of choice was the Belgian Malinois, preferred over the German Shepherd for its adaptability to changes in environment and acceptance of new owners. Then, too, Dixieland was not forgotten by our first black mayors, who insisted that German Shepherds not be employed by SCMPD.

Our K-9 Unit began training in August 2001, pairing Sergeant Haysman with K-9 Nero, Corporal Ernst with K-9 Bruno, Corporal Dukarski with K-9 Nick, and Corporal McGruder with K-9 Binky. The dogs were trained to detect and were certified to locate marijuana, cocaine, heroin, and methamphetamine. They were also trained to patrol and track, search and apprehend suspects, locate evidence, and were adept at climbing ladders, jumping through windows and crawling through tight spaces.

APO Joe Groover joined the K-9 Unit and took over handling K-9 Nero when Sergeant Haysman left SCMPD to join the active National Guard. Ernie was promoted to Sergeant in 2003, remaining with the Unit until promoted to Lieutenant in 2013. APO Mike Drayton and K-9 Chip joined the team in 2004, bringing the number of teams to 5 when EXPO came into being. Chris Amedee and K-9 Lakia joined the Unit late in 2006, bringing the final count to 6 teams.

I had worked with all of the dogs and their handlers prior to EXPO. They were a damn good group of officers, including the ones with four legs. Dukarski and Nick were always there whenever I called for K-9 on the radio. McGruder and Drayton were the same way, even if they were more liability conscious. Before letting the dogs loose they wanted a complete rundown on the stop. I mistakenly thought they were sharp-shooting my methods until I found out they were simply trying to help me make better stops.

* * * * *

The first organizational meeting for EXPO was held at the Chatham County Annex, also known as Precinct 1-- the old Chatham County Police Headquarters-- near I-16. We gathered in the Rose Greene Room, named for a County Lieutenant who had been ill and died in office. Sergeant Capers reiterated what he had said to each of us on the phone: we were the alpha males of SCMPD and we had been chosen to take the fight to enemy territory, to jump corners and kick ass.

We are not here to bother the workingman, Capers admonished us. *We do not bother old dudes and the longshoremen unless they are wrong. When you treat people good and fair, you develop friends and informants, and you can never have too many of either. Treat people right and the guy you let off for joint might one day tip you off on a murder.*

Then Capers made the one statement that made the greatest impression on me. He said, *Fellas, we are going to go out and get these guys. We are going to take the fight to them. But remember one thing:*

32

these boys have rights. We are going to come within an inch of them, but they have rights and don't you forget it.

And then, as if to underscore what Capers had said, he introduced Cameron Ippolito from the United States Attorney's Office, who spoke to us about Operation Ceasefire, and Daryle McCormick, our liaison with the local Bureau of Alcohol, Tobacco, Firearms and Explosives. I knew then and there that EXPO was going to be about guns and getting them off the streets. I love getting guns off the streets and out of the hands of people who have no respect for the law.

I looked around the room at the other members of the squad, few of whom I knew personally but every single one by reputation, and realized that we had the makings of a unit that could take down more dope and recover more weapons than the rest of the department combined.

Tim "Lew" Lewis and Anthony "Mac" McBride came to EXPO from the West Chatham Precinct crime suppression unit, aggressive guys who roamed the more active parts of the territory. Lew did not shy away from physical confrontation with suspects who were less than compliant with his lawful commands. He may have been young but he was 6-ft. tall and tipped the scales at 245, and could hold his own in the street. Mac had a similar, no nonsense approach to the street.

Terrence Zearing and Jeff Oliver also came out of West Chatham to EXPO. Z, like me, was an army veteran, military police, who found out that there was a whole different way to police once he joined EXPO. Oliver was the son of the retired chief of Chatham County police prior to

33

the merger; the apple did not fall far from the tree. Oliver was the strong, silent type and had law enforcement in his blood.

In forming EXPO, Sergeant Capers practically emptied out the talent pool from Central Precinct, traditionally the most active hotspot in Savannah: Anderson Street to DeRenne Avenue and Truman Parkway to Ogeechee Road. Most of the high crime areas rest within these boundaries. Cuyler-Brownsville, Hazzard County, Seiler Avenue are all open-air drug markets and a shooting gallery of violent crime. David Branch and Chris Talley came out of Central. Talley was a college boy out of Ohio, with a year on the street and with no overt issues with self-confidence. He had good speed and an abundance of energy. Jeron Young had completed his probationary period and was working afternoon shift in Central when he got the call from Capers. A Marine to his core, Young very much looked the part of a squared away troop and was attending college at the same time. Terrance Jackson, Darrin Mitchell, Floyd Sawyer and EXPO's Big Dawg Rufus Brown also came from Central. By the time this book is done, you will know all you need to know about these guys.

Capers went Downtown to find his fireplugs. Home to Savannah's vaunted Historic District and nightlife, the tourist industry thrives there and so does the drug trade. Downtown Precinct is home to the biggest housing projects in Savannah, notorious for spawning the drug trade and violent crime, especially the 500 blocks of Bolton, Waldberg, Park and Duffy streets, along with the Ben Van Clark neighborhood.

Josh Hunt was an up and coming star with the department having done his training and probationary period in Central Precinct and recruited to strengthen B-Watch, where we met and became partners. Hunt was a natural leader with high energy, the perfect combination of physical skill and mental prowess. We made the perfect pairing, on and off the field of battle. For every shift I spent working alongside Hunt, I became a better officer. I always knew he would not remain with SCMPD forever. He was bound for bigger and better things.

Lorenza Baker came to EXPO from the Islands Precinct. He had a nose for dope and the speed to catch it, probably one of the fastest humans I have ever seen. Kelvin Frazier would come from the Islands also.

Randy Veal came out of Southside Precinct. A Desert Storm Veteran, Veal was a high-strung guy who gladly traded the quiet side of town for the aggressive patrol of EXPO. Though it took a couple of Months, Randy Smith came out of the Southside too. Randy made his mark when he arrived also.

In the year that followed, EXPO became famous. There were officers not assigned to the Unit that wanted to be, officers who were not assigned to the unit and did not want to be, and officers of every stripe, rank and ability that would come to have an opinion on EXPO and how we operated. We made big arrests-- lawful arrests-- and we made a lot of them. It was all done by the book and we grew together as a unit. We pushed the edge of the envelope to the limit and checked with supervisors and district attorneys to make sure things were done correctly. Rumors about bad cases, needless and excessive beatings, or malicious and illegal searches were all untrue, mostly started by officers who wanted to see EXPO fail.

It was no secret that Chief Lovett and Sergeant Capers were friends. I do not know a thing about their friendship except that it had begun when Capers was just a kid and Mr. Lovett was the cop on his beat. I heard whispers to the effect that the only reason Capers rose to his position with EXPO was because of that friendship but I know that was not the only reason. Greg Capers was a cop, a real cop.

I heard other rumors about Capers double dipping by taking off-duty jobs while on the clock. I knew something about his domestic situation that ultimately would be his undoing. I know that Greg Capers is not a perfect man but I also know he is my friend. Our friendship developed over the years of good times and bad, and it all began with EXPO.

The only reason Sergeant Capers selected me for EXPO was because he wanted Hunt and when he asked Hunt if he had anyone else who was up for this kind of unit, Hunt gave him my name. Capers then called Sergeant Tamargo, who vouched for me, and Sergeant Rowse seconded the motion.

Tamargo had shown me how to police and Capers let me go out and do it. Capers was always the first to break his foot off in my ass when I screwed up but was quick to pick me up, dust me off and get me back in The Game. He gave me opportunities to do things in police work that I am most proud of. And he prepared us for supervisory positions long before we were eligible for promotion by introducing us to project logs and administrative functions and giving each member of EXPO the chance to run our shift for the night.

Greg Capers was the type of leader I aspired to be when I was a non-commissioned officer in the Army and the type of officer I wanted to be in SCMPD. He was a magician when it came to handling the egos of the thoroughbred stallions that made up his unit and was innovative in the way he paired underperformers with guys operating at higher levels. To top it off, Greg Capers was no pussy. He did not back down from a challenge and when alpha males puffed out their chest to get their way, he blew back and we respected him for it. Capers was not afraid to let us succeed because he understood that is what leaders do. He understood that our success was a direct reflection of his leadership: he provided the tools and we did the job. Ultimately, like myself, his personal life was his undoing. But make no mistake about it, Greg Capers is a good man and was a hell of a cop.

Sergeant Capers needed guys who did not need to be told where to go or what to do in smoking out the criminal element. He needed officers that wanted to work and needed no additional motivation. He did not want guys who showed up for 40 hours, rode around and participated only when necessary. He needed meat eaters. He wanted guys who hit the streets running, knowing where to go, what they were looking for and how to get it. He needed the best street cops in the county and so he went out and got them. Guys that did not need to be followed in order to make sure they were doing the right thing when no one was looking.

The best explanation I have ever heard about this type of police work came from Sergeant Mike Robbins, and Old School cop who knew what it takes to police a city. Robbins explained that there is a difference between a cop and a CPO-- Career Police Officer. A cop makes a difference and is not afraid to mix it up with the bad guys; a Career Police officer picks off the easy targets, rides calls and writes reports.

Sergeant Robbins did not have much need for the CPO's in SCMPD; Sergeant Capers had none.

At the same time EXPO was formed, most of the precincts in SCMPD had Crime Suppression Units (CSU). All of them folded, except the Narcotics Eradication Team (NET) in Central Precinct, because of the significant amount of manpower that was pulled for EXPO. (NET was actually part of the Criminal Investigative Division so they were not affected by what Patrol was doing.) This created a lot of bad blood among officers who were passed over for EXPO and those who had no interest in leaving their present assignments.

The Downtown Special Operation Unit (DSO) was the most effective CSU up to this point and its dissolution was a big hit to the precinct and to morale. George Gundich was a member of DSO at the time, a hardheaded legit tough guy fresh out of Ranger Battalion at Hunter Army Airfield. George kept at his job and put together a string of effective units over the years. I later worked for him after his promotion to Sergeant and I learned a lot from Gundich, especially when things did not go his way and he simply drove on. Ashley Brown and Dave Arbizo operated in a similar fashion.

The CSU uniform was the Department Class C outfit: black Battle Dress Uniform style pants and yellow polo style shirts with a black screen printed badge on the left chest and POLICE in large black letters across the back. Pistol belt and black boots rounded out the outfit that became identifiable on the streets as our aggressive reputation made us increasingly unpopular among gangs. EXPO was distinctive, noticeable and as notorious as any gang in its black and yellow colors.

When the Yellow Shirts were out, all the other gangs would learn to stay in.

Of course, our opponents were clever people who lived by their wits. Criminals, for the most part, have well run operations complete with lookouts and corner boys. Any neighborhood big enough to have a name is big enough to have a gang to control its turf and, yes, there are several Savannah gangs that have ties to nationwide criminal organizations. In time, after we had hit them hard enough, we had to devise clever ways to sneak up on drug dealers. At the first sight of a Yellow Shirt, street corner set ups were shut down.

EXPO was always on the street. We did not have an office to sit around and sip coffee and we never stood still waiting for a call. Our schedule often changed from days to afternoons, with Sundays and Mondays off, and we were given a few days notice when the change would occur. It was a moot point for me personally because I could not wait to get out there-- daytime, nighttime, it did not matter. I just wanted to be there when shit went down.

It is a widespread misconception that crime only occurs at night and on weekends. There is always something going down in Savannah, and to catch it cops have to be willing and hungry enough to find it.

EXPO was always hungry.

Chapter Three

It's understood, I do it for the hood

For every EXPO shift, my partner J-Hunt and I started our day doing stretches behind the Annex after roll call. We wanted to be ready for anything and everything from the jump off. We had developed a craving for a citrus energy drink called Full Throttle, jacked with enough vitamin B, sugar and caffeine to wire a racehorse, and which we picked up at the first convenience store we encountered, and then headed to our first area of operation. We loved that stuff so much that sometimes we held off buying the first round until after the first arrest, as a reward and incentive.

Right from the start Rufus Brown and Floyd Sawyer were the lead dawgs in our pack. Yeah, their names sounded like they were soul singers, but in reality they were heavy-hitting guys from the toughest precinct in a town festering in crime. To say Brown and Sawyer understood the streets of Savannah is to make a massive understatement.

Let me tell you about Rufus Brown. Pay careful attention, please:

He is the quintessential quiet giant, as wide as he is tall, and a Combat Veteran who once rode a Bradley Fighting Vehicle during Operation Desert Storm. He had grown up in Hudson Hill on the west side of Savannah, which most white people could not find with a map and a compass nor venture into without police escort. He was a grandfather but he was still in good enough shape to run down fleeing teenagers with ease. He held no official rank among the rank and file yet he was the undisputed leader of EXPO. He spoke only when absolutely necessary and when he did, everyone listened; his actions spoke even louder for themselves.

His ability to formulate strategies for attacking street corners is what set EXPO apart from all other crime suppression units that had come before and would undoubtedly follow. At a time when the title has been watered down, bastardized and misused, Rufus Brown is a bona fide hero. He is my hero. I will state here and now for the record that I would not have accomplished anything exceptional in police work had I not the benefit of working with Rufus Brown. He was then, and at the time of this writing, the best street cop in Savannah.

Rufus Brown gets up before dawn and crawls under a blighted house on the corner of the dodgiest part of town and waits and watches what transpires for twelve hours without moving or making a sound. No one orders him to do it. He does it to gain his own intel. I don't know if you have ever been to Savannah, Georgia in the summer but laying under a house in sweltering heat takes dedication on a level few understand. And he does it because driving by in an unmarked car that has been made by every gang banger just doesn't cut it in neighborhoods like Cuyler-Brownsville.

Floyd Sawyer, like Rufus Brown, was a powerhouse standing 5-foot-8 and 250 pounds of solid muscle. He was a light-skinned brother with hazel eyes and a baldhead, and the conduit that made the core of EXPO work so well. He was a street-savvy Savannahian that grew up in the Garden Homes housing project, went off to college to play baseball, and ended up with a masters degree from Savannah State. That he had no fear and a deadly sense of humor made him one of our Most Valuable Players.

Brown and Sawyer conducted scads of field interviews and traffic stops; it is what we did. If they saw something that did not look right, they stopped and addressed it. They were as hungry if not hungrier than J-Hunt and I. Sometimes they just said hello and sometimes they stopped because the activity warranted detaining a suspect to find out what they were up to. Whatever the case, Brown and Sawyer were all over it.

One night while roaming West Chatham Precinct, Brown and Sawyer stopped a subject at Scarborough and Augusta Avenue, then as now a well-known drug store of the open-air variety. They had stopped him because he was standing in the middle of the street without any apparent reason for doing so. Brown spoke to him while the subject nibbled at a slice of pizza. They went through the typical field interview for pertinent information and Sawyer relayed it to Records to check for outstanding warrants and probation notices. It was at this moment that Officer Shauna Williams arrived as backup. Shauna was one of my training officers from the Downtown Precinct who worked overtime with EXPO while we were starting up.

Sawyer returned from his car and asked the subject to repeat his name because all of his information was coming up blank. The reader may find this hard to believe but it is relatively common for subjects to lie about their identity to police. The subject repeated the name he had given Sawyer and Shauna overheard the exchange.

That's not his name, Shauna said to Sawyer. *His name is Bruce*.

And it was at this point that Bruce decided to break off from the field interview, offering the remainder of his pizza to Sawyer by throwing it at him, and went for a run. He did not get far; that's typically what happened when subjects ran from Brown; Sawyer was never far behind.

Typical days with EXPO were two man units. We rode together in vehicles that were assigned to the team. Every so often however, the bigger guys would jam themselves in a van that had the same markings as a patrol vehicle with lights and everything. It was a big white van, looked like something schools would use to transport football teams. Large clear windows and space to move around. This van however got loaded with some of the biggest guys on the unit. Brown, Sawyer, Lewis, Frazier, Oliver and whoever else could fit all piled in. This gave them the ability to deploy a huge payload when they arrived on a target. Because of the size of this payload we affectionately dubbed it, The Meat Wagon.

J Hunt and I chose to ride around in our Dodge Intrepid most of the time but if there was a day that one of us was tied up we were not shy to jump in the Meat Wagon. One day J Hunt jumped in and they headed to the Victorian District. This used to be Hunt's beat and so he was always ahead of The Game when it came to where to look and the ability to direct other units toward the activity he spotted. J-Hunt knew this neighborhood cold.

There were some gentlemen congregating on a porch at the corner of Habersham and Park, too close for comfort to comfortable houses. J-Hunt made contact with a big dude standing on the front steps of a less fashionable residence and all the other guys who did not want to be sociable ran inside. J-Hunt was trying to talk to the big dude who was now blocking the line of sight into the house and refusing to comply with lawful orders to stand aside.

Rufus Brown showed up in support, quickly surveyed the scene, and ran toward J-Hunt, picking him up on the fly as Hunt goes plank, and used him like a battering ram to knock over the big dude. All three of them crashed through the front door and into the house. Everyone was secured and a stolen pistol was recovered.

I have seen a lot of incredible things in my time but I never saw anything like Rufus Brown turning J-Hunt into a battering ram and breaking down a door, not even in Jason Statham movies.

One night early into the operation, Josh and I were riding the Downtown Precinct and slipped through the lanes to see if anything was stirring. Lanes being a common place for suspects to hide and avoid detection, the City of Savannah has an ordinance forbidding use of the lanes as a thoroughfare unless the subject is a resident or visiting one of the properties.

We searched the lanes near the Civic Center and Orleans Square, the EXPO epicenter, otherwise known as The Square Where Jennifer Ross Was Killed. We pulled into Perry Lane and J-Hunt saw that the iron gate to the carriage house at 124 ½ was wide open. This being near the scene of the Ross homicide, we decided to stop and check on the property. I thought maybe the gate had been left open but when approaching we could see the door to the residence was also wide open and the unmistakable stank of burnt marijuana was wafting into the lane from inside. As we moved in for a closer look, a young man met us at the

44

door and, surprise, he had the same unmistakable stank emanating from his person.

Inside there were two companions in the living room and on the counter in plain sight was a gun. The subjects jumped up from their comfy seats at the same time we moved in to prevent them from getting to the gun. Now we could see a pill bottle packed with stems and a blue jewelry bag containing white powder. Time now for one of our patented field interviews with the greeter during which we recovered a black bag packed with several plastic bags of grass and a scale indicating that these fine gentlemen were in the distribution business.

The kicker was that one of these gentlemen who was up to his ass in this drug business was walking through Orleans Square with Jennifer Ross when they were accosted on Christmas Eve.

I will remind the reader that at this particular point in time the Ross Murder was still an open investigation and the four assailants had not been found.

So J-Hunt and I made the calls that resulted in SCPL Randy Powell dropping by with his evidence kit and together we packaged and processed the contraband. Powell was out of the Islands Precinct, a retired Army Staff Sergeant with a vast amount of experience in traffic enforcement. Seeing how much evidence was flooding into headquarters in the first few weeks of Operation EXPO, Powell saw a way to expedite the process by assembling an evidence collection kit and filled it with bags, tape, envelopes, test kits and forms for filing evidence.

We called Sarge so that he could notify command that we were onto something big in the biggest case on the department's books. We charged one of the suspects and left the rest to detectives who arrived quickly on the scene to take over.

Shortly after this night, Sarge informed us that Sergeant Schaff, the TRAP (Vice Unit) Supervisor, had received a tip from an informant that the vehicle used as a getaway car in the Ross Murder was on the racks at a mechanic shop on Wheaton Street.

EXPO accompanied Sergeant Schaff to the location and found a Ford Taurus matching the description of the getaway car. There was a bunch of guys hanging out that had no apparent purpose for being in this place of business. Officer Darren Mitchell made contact with one of the subjects and the next thing I know Mitchell had him in cuffs after finding a couple of baggies filled with cocaine on him. Supervisors arrived and brought CNT with them. Not only did we find more cocaine, we mined enough information out of the subjects to establish that the car in question was the getaway car.

Detectives were now that much closer to solving the Ross Murder.

Officer Mitchell was one of the guys that made EXPO more of an experience than just another CSU. He was coming off having been named Officer of the Year by the Savannah Exchange Club when he was invited to join EXPO. He had a reputation for being extremely aggressive and was not shy about his attributes, typically greeting strangers with his resume. But he had an instinct for the streets that I cannot begin to describe, except to say that I was jealous of his ability to know that

46

something was amiss. It was like he had some sort of psychic ability. He could feel trouble in his bones. There was madness in his methods and artistry in the way he articulated his stops. His greatest statement in Recorder's Court was the day that he told the Assistant District Attorney that he had stopped a suspect because "he looked dirty".

The rest of the Ross Murder came together quickly and on January 31, Michael Thorpe was arrested and charged with the crime. More arrests followed. The vehicle we found at the shop was traced to Kevin Huckabee. Detectives got the rest of the story from Sean Thorpe, Michael's uncle, who was granted immunity in exchange for his testimony detailing how he and Michael and Webster Wilson and Kevin Huckabee trolled for an easy target to rob and spotted a group of inebriated college kids near Perry Lane at 3 o'clock in the morning and couldn't resist. District Attorney Spencer Lawton tapped Assistant District Attorney Christy Barker to handle the prosecution of the case.

Christy Barker is one of the best prosecutors I have ever seen in a courtroom, short of Karl Knoche, an Assistant United States Attorney for the Southern District of Georgia, maybe the best. Christy was more assertive and better prepared than any attorney I ever knew, and in my career I've testified in hundreds of cases. Hundreds.

The trial was nationally televised on Court TV in December 2006. Michael Thorpe, Webster Wilson and Kevin Huckabee were convicted of the murder of Jennifer Ross and Savannah had its revenge.

It was a diligent effort, Chief Lovett said of the arrests in the Ross case. *The officers did a terrific job thanks to, in part, the community, with what tips that they gave and the information they*

47

provided us, which enabled us to do this. I want to stress that this was a joint effort between the community and the police, he said.

Chief Lovett was master of the moment, hitting all the right notes in thanking the public who thanked him right back for a job well done. Oh, the town felt ever so much better about their new Chief, and the next thing we knew he was sitting in a place of honor at the big table down front at the Savannah Rotary Club luncheon held at that bastion of gentility, the DeSoto Hilton, where on many occasions he was the only tan face in the room that wasn't waiting tables.

Broughton Street went back to business, tourists packed the trolleys, Hollywood camped out in our squares.

And what of the Shante Cooper Murder, the reader may ask?

I'll bet the reader has forgotten all about her in just 29 pages, just like the rest of Savannah, back in 2006.

Well, the first leads in the Cooper Murder did not begin to trickle into the Department until years after she was buried. EXPO had come and gone and Josh Hunt had been moved to Homicide.

J-Hunt had not forgotten Shante Cooper.

It could have happened to anybody, Hunt told the newspaper. *Something like that drives you to do everything you can, because this was somebody's mother and daughter, and she was loved by her family and the community.*

Shante is still loved, Josh told the press, *and we wanted to do everything we can to honor that.*

After three years and four months from the date of her murder, the first of three people involved in her senseless killing was arrested and the identities of the other two was revealed.

But by tracking down the killers of Jennifer Ross and bringing them to justice in less than a year, Chief Willie Lovett, SCMPD and EXPO let it be known that crime would not pay in Savannah, Georgia, at least not in the historic district. Pursuit of criminals would be urgent, trials would be speedy, and justice would be served. The business elite could breathe easier, even more tourists continued to pour into town, and locals were pleasantly distracted by all of the Hollywood stars.

As for EXPO, we were racking up arrests and the team was coming together as a fighting unit. One of my favorite stories about EXPO exploits occurred shortly after the Ross case was shelved:

We were operating in an area that I dubbed Seabrook Village, named for a prominent family that had been involved in criminal activity for generations like it was the family business. Everybody else called the neighborhood Edgemere/Sackville, which has long been and continues to be a high crime area. Brown and Sawyer were rolling on the 1100 block of East 55th Street when they spotted a subject leaning into the passenger side of a car like there was a drug deal going on. The occupants of the car looked up and saw Brown watching them and the leaning subject straightened up and took off running. Brown was right behind him.

Running through yards and hurdling fences, the chase continued for several minutes. Sawyer called out the chase like a racetrack announcer at Churchill Downs and the rest of EXPO flooded into the area. What I saw next is unforgettable:

The subject was losing steam, like a scene from National Geographic TV when a lion is bearing down on its prey. He was plumb tuckered out and had run up on one fence too many, and out of exhaustion decided not to jump. He turned and faced the charging Rufus and grabbed his waistband as if he were going for a weapon. Brown did not break stride, planting his foot in the kid's chest and the two of them went through the fence together.

The kid kept his hands in his waistband even as Brown tried to get the suspect's arms behind his back and cuff him. Hauling the kid to his feet, Brown found a 9mm pistol, a pocketful of cash and another pocket filled with marijuana. This, however, was no ordinary kid. This was Sidney Grant, also known as Tre-4, who would go on to become one of Savannah's most infamous killers.

Sidney and his brother Michael aka Faye Mike grew up in Hitch Village. When Faye Mike was murdered, Tre-4 didn't take it well and I suspect this is where he began his quest. Tre-4 became one of Savannah's most notorious killers and this was the first time I had witnessed him being arrested. The last time I would see him would be in 2013, right around St. Patrick's Day, laying in the middle of Indian Street, covered by a white sheet in front of Club Inferno. At the time of his death, Tre-4 was the lead suspect in no less than five murders, including one of Savannah's biggest red balls: the Emily Pickles and Michael Biancasino Murders. Another white girl and the brother of a

50

prominent ambulance chaser; I think I've previously mentioned how much Savannah hates that.

Tre-4 is the only murder victim I ever saw that as he lay in a pool of blood a police Major, Homicide Sergeant and Homicide Detective stood over him smiling.

Later I talked to an informant about Tre-4's murder and the kid said something I will never forget: *I was shocked he ain't just spontaneously combust right there*, the informant said. *That niggah was pure evil.*

* * * * *

EXPO haunted West Savannah out of respect for Sergeant Capers and his old stomping grounds. Clearview was a hub of our operations and we were never on site long before something broke out.

David Brand called out that he was in hot pursuit on foot. Chris Talley was with him and they were headed west. I moved along the backside of The Alamo Plaza and spotted a subject shedding his clothes as fast as he could, a common tactic of suspects who need to change their appearance quickly. EXPO swarmed the complex and Yellow Shirts were flying in every direction between the narrow spaces of buildings that make up the neighborhood so that we looked like one great big game of Pac Man on steroids.

The suspect was apprehended near the playground and Dave doubled back to find a jacket the suspect had discarded and found a packet of crack rocks, 49, if memory serves me correctly.

The suspect was a kid I had run into before known as Smurf. His real name was Freddie Early. This was the beginning of young Fred's criminal career. The last time I would peep Smurf was in 2013, as he was being loaded onto the back of an ambulance at Richards and Eagle streets, suffering from multiple gunshot wounds, along with two side chicks, also suffering from the same malady. The girls survived; Smurf did not.

Dave makes a better story: Dave and I were hired and went to the Academy together. I remember the day we met, sharing a bench in the lobby of Colonel Oliver's office awaiting our final interviews, the last stop in the hiring process. Exchanging the usual pleasantries, we discovered we were Yankees. He was born in Pittsburgh and raised in New York, and had gone to a small private school in Connecticut nobody ever heard of called Loomis Chaffee. I was the only person Dave had ever met that knew Loomis Chaffee and that's because I grew up three blocks from its main campus in my hometown of Windsor. Dave and I became instant friends then and there.

Dave did not act like it but Dave came from money. He did not have to be a cop. He went to Hobart College, which had been founded in 1822 in the Finger Lakes Region of New York State, and routinely turns out the kind of students that win prestigious fellowships like the Rhodes, Gates Cambridge, Udall, Fulbright and Goldwater. But the Military was in Dave's blood, dating all the way back to a great-great-great named Thomas Posey, who had been an officer in the American Revolution and promoted to General. Dave had in mind joining the Air Force, then changed course when he received an ROTC scholarship, joining the Marine Corps prior to joining SCMPD.

Dave might've been a little fucker but he was not afraid to box outside his weight with any challenger and had a strong thirst for street level crime fighting.

The intersection of Clinch and Stark on the westside of town became a honey hole for EXPO. J-Hunt and I would be cruising Tatumville, the meat wagon would deliver its hidden payload of Yellow Shirts that pounced on anything that moved or was suspicious. But my partner and I never ventured out that way for the simple fact that if Brown, Sawyer, Lewis and Frazier could not handle whatever they happened upon, J-Hunt and I were not going to be the deciding factor. One of the first bingos hit by EXPO was an arrest made by the heavy hitters who jumped out on a group of guys gathered out front of their makeshift studio where they were burning pirated CDs and movies. They talked to the subjects long enough to discover several pounds of marijuana in an SUV parked out front.

J-Hunt and I were damn comfortable riding together. We had been involved in foot chases in the Downtown Precinct that I usually started and he usually finished, fast little bastard, but I finished a few of them for him, too. We worked exceedingly well together to the point where I could see where he was going during a stop before he went there. Truth be told, J-Hunt was a great partner but he was the worst passenger I have ever driven. If I turned right, he would insist we should have gone left. If we were heading toward a dispatched call or EXPO alert, according to him, I went the wrong way.

We compiled a playlist of our favorite tunes that kept up our spirits while riding around: T.I., Trick Daddy and Young Jeezy. We cued up "I Do It For the 'Hood" several times per shift and it always got us fired up like it was the soundtrack to our existence.

But the thing we had most in common-- aside from impeccable taste in music-- was that we could feel where we should be. The reader may laugh and think that is a load of crap, but it is true. J-Hunt had an uncanny instinct for trouble that was rivaled only by Rufus Brown and Darrin Mitchell. We were both high energy guys and tremendously competitive and, unlike any other team I have ever seen or been partnered, we truly wanted to do better than the other teams. This was the strength of EXPO: the majority of us were competitors.

If Rufus went out and made an arrest, it made us want to go out and get two. If Frazier got a guy with crack, we wanted a gun. And the rest of EXPO fed off of us in the same way. In the process we made each other better. We did not sharp-shoot what other teammates were doing. If they did it well, we tried harder to do better.

It was unnecessary for our supervising captain or the other command staff to come down hard on EXPO; we had a way of policing ourselves. One night when the meat wagon rolled through the 700 block of Waters Avenue, we spotted a crew standing in front of row houses that were notorious outlets for drugs and a nest of other quality of life issues. The meat wagon dropped its load of Yellow Shirts and the crew scattered. Everyone secured a suspect, with the lone exception of one member of the team who left one of the suspects untouched. This was highly unusual and uncharacteristic of EXPO. To make matters worse, when Rufus went over and secured the remaining suspect he turned out to be armed; this did not sit well with the team.

54

The next day at roll call, Sergeant Capers ran down his usual briefing and then cut us loose. But not before Rufus told Sarge that we needed a closed-door session.

Okay, said Sarge, and closed the door.

Sarge, we need you on the other side of that door, Rufus said. *This is between us.*

Capers copped an inquisitive look but knew when he was not wanted or needed. He stepped outside and closed the door behind him.

Then Rufus said, *Hey, look, this is a highly aggressive unit. When we jump out, we ain't jumpin' out to make friends.*

Everybody nodded in agreement.

If you ain't built to put your hands on people, Rufus continued, *this might not be the unit for you.*

An uneasy feeling crept over the room.

If a suspect is left unsecured while your brothers are otherwise engaged and can't see what's going on behind them, the whole group is vulnerable, Rufus said, *and we can't have that.*

No one had anything to add; the Big Man had said it all. He didn't have to get personal and he didn't have to get ugly. He kept it real and everybody understood exactly what he meant.

The next day, the teammate that had come up short at the hit and run on Waters Avenue requested that he be sent back to his old precinct. There was no shame in it. Not everyone is built for this type of work.

No one is doing this type of work in Savannah now.

*   *   *   *   *

We were back in Central Precinct. "Ridin' Dirty" was playing over the speakers. Heading out East 39th Street, J-Hunt ejected from the car before I knew what was going on. Dave was hauling ass and Rufus was in front of them. I jumped out and took out after them. All I could see was that the guy we were chasing had a head start and was fast as hell. I don't know what sport he played in school but I would've wanted him on my team; a shame, really, that he was playing for the other side now.

It was an unusual case in that the suspect stayed in a straight line. He must've counted on the fact that he was faster than us and that the shortest distance between two points is a straight line. And he may have been fast on his feet but no one can outrun the radio. That is not to say that we caught everyone that ever ran from us. But it required a certain amount of speed and misdirection to get away. Stay on the same course that is radioed in and there is nothing tricky about back up units getting ahead and cutting off the suspect. And let that be a lesson to the reader.

But this cut off was a shocker: After what seemed like a marathon of a foot chase, I looked towards MLK, across the median separating north and southbound lanes, where the streetlights were brighter because the tree canopy opens up onto an intersection of two major arteries, and where the pursuit ended with a resounding thud. The suspect's feet went straight up in the air and his body hit the ground forcefully, causing him to make a high-pitched shriek that echoed through my mind to this day. The suspect, Jaquez Baker aka Peanut, had been taken into custody and was lying on the sidewalk in handcuffs when I got there. A metro patrol car was in the southbound lane and I saw old Fred Hill dusting himself off after having delivered the hit of a lifetime on Peanut, the high point of his highlight reel.

Fred was a mountain of a man who worked the Southside Precinct as an assistant patrol supervisor, a quiet and relaxed kind of guy, a stark contrast to the aggressive style of a Greg Capers. Fred did not rile easily, but when he riled, he did not take any shit off anyone, which served him well when having to deal with loud and energetic Type-A personalities on EXPO. I did not know Fred Hill when EXPO began but I came to respect him over the eleven months we worked together.

After the shockwaves of Fred's monster hit subsided and the arrest had set in, I heard Peanut yelling like a madman and saw him rolling around like he was on fire. Nobody had laid a finger on him and I thought for a minute that the drugs must be kicking in. As a matter of fact he was on fire of sorts: he was lying in a bed of fire ants. It took a minute or two for the ants to get down to business but they made a feast out of Peanut.

We cleaned up Peanut before presenting him to his jailers and this was the only memorable contact I had with him, face to face anyway. Dave Brand had far more encounters with Peanut than I did and said that Peanut ran from him and his partner so many times they had to choose who would chase him next.

Peanut became a sort of legend in Cuyler-Brownsville in 2009, when he was shot 36 times in a setup that settled the matter of who was in charge of selling crack in CBV.

After we had finished cleaning up Peanut on this occasion, J-Hunt and I were released for lunch. I vividly remember Sarge looking at me and telling me we were cut loose and to lay low while we ate. So we headed down Montgomery on our way to a well-deserved break when I see a guy creeping in West Waldburg Lane.

J-Hunt took a hard left into the lane and we approached the subject who had that familiar which-way-should-I-run look about him and reflexively went to his pockets, telegraphing that he was holding something he shouldn't, and backed away from us. I closed the gap to keep him from leaving in a hurry and positioned him between me and Josh and our unit. The subject continued to fidget and grab himself for something.

Put your hands on the hood of the car, I commanded.

He was trying to be cooperative at the same time he was all hyped up.

I patted him down and felt a short cylinder that felt like glass with jagged edges, the outlines of what by now I was able to identify as a crack pipe. I asked him if that was what I thought it was and he reached into his right pants pocket. I was sure it was a stem but could not swear to it in court. Then the suspect slapped my hand away and I advised him not to do it again. He nodded in affirmation that the object was in fact contraband.

58

I thought he was trying to be helpful when he reached in to grab it. I stopped him and told him to keep his hands on the car and that I would remove it. As I reached into his pocket and grabbed the pipe, he reached and grabbed my hand while shrieking into my ear.

I thought that was an odd thing to do. J-Hunt concurred and radioed Dispatch that we had a situation that was escalating from pat down to throw down. The ack-ack of radio chatter caused the suspect to struggle and I felt the jagged edges of the stem cut into the palm of my hand.

He cut me, I said

My partner was on the suspect in an instant, pummeling him with a barrage of blows which only caused the pipe to dig deeper into my hand. At this point Hunt had no idea what I had been cut with. Once we got the suspect in cuffs I retrieved the pipe but found nothing else on him. All that anguish for a lousy misdemeanor possession but because there was a significant use of force, I also charged him with felony Obstruction. I hated putting a charge like that on the guy because, in my mind, what he was doing wasn't a felony. He was obviously geeked up but I couldn't justify the use of force without the accompanying charge. That's just how it goes sometimes.

Sergeant Capers, who had heard the news go out over the radio, arrived at the scene none too happy, with that look of disapproval for which he was famous.

I know, I told him. I couldn't help myself, I said.

59

It never worked but it was all I had. Sarge had told us to break bread and lay low and we disobeyed a direct order. But when wired like J-Hunt and I are built, we could not help ourselves. We reacted purely out of instinct and sense of duty. But Sarge was pissed that his officer was now headed for Emergency to get inspected, neglected, further injected and hopefully disinfected for whatever had been implanted into my hand, and would be lost for the remainder of the afternoon. I loaded up on my least favorite cocktails for Hepatitis A, Series B, Rabies and Tetanus, just to be sure.

Given that the suspect was charged with felony obstruction, we had to be in court for his arraignment and preliminary hearing so that bond could be considered. My partner and I rode the bench in the back row of the courtroom where we customarily sat and waited our turn. All of the defendants had front row seats. I did not see our guy.

Watch, Josh said to me. *They're gonna wheel him in on a stretcher or some shit.*

No sooner than the prediction escaped his lips the door leading to the holding cell swings open and the Deputies assigned to the court pushed our guy into the gallery in a wheelchair. He had on a neck brace and was scuffed up in ways we had not seen.

The assistant ditrict attorney invited me to the stage. I mean the witness stand. We had performed this duet so many times it was like Greg Jacobs and I were in harmony. He knew what to ask and I knew what to answer and we had it down to a fine science. Greg Jacobs was a highly talented and brilliant prosecutor. I only ever remember seeing

60

him handle the Recorder's Court dockets but it was always clear to me that he was the top dog in the DA's Office and he always offered his opinions on how to best make a case.

I do not remember the entire prelim if only because the hundreds I testified in seem to run together as time goes by. But I do remember the following exchange with the defendant's attorney:

Do you recognize the defendant my client?

Yes, I replied.

Was the defendant in a wheelchair when you apprehended him in West Waldburg Lane, officer?

No, I replied.

The attorney, with all the righteous indignation he could muster, fired at me: *Then why is the defendant my client in a wheelchair now?*

I don't know, I said. *I'm not a doctor.*

*   *   *   *   *

Downtown and Central Precincts were home base for J-Hunt and I. If we ventured too far east we were like rookies searching for street signs and landmarks. Knowing where we were at all times was one of the most important factors in keeping safe; hard for back up to get to us if we do not know where we are.

61

Case in point: We were prowling around Savannah High School and as we drove past a parked van I spotted a guy crouching next to it with that I-hope-they-don't-see-me look on his face. But we saw him and I did not have to say a word. J-Hunt stopped the car as my foot hit the ground. The suspect took off and I called on the radio, got one running. And we were off to the races.

The three of us jumped fences like this was some sort of urban track meet. I am on the radio letting other units in the vicinity know that we are in pursuit on foot.

We are around the house, I hollered.

The other units hollered back, *what house*?

The house on the corner, I hollered.

What corner?!

I have no clue, I said, and clicked off so that I could concentrate on catching the leader.

We must've run around the same fucking house ten fucking times before I pulled the patented Wiley Coyote move by stopping and waiting for the suspect to come around again. As he took the corner, he stopped and changed direction. Not the best choice because J-Hunt had not halted and I felt the collision when cop met robber. 10-95, chase concluded. Resistance ceased. And that is how it usually played out.

It really is a Game, you know, this cops and robbers thing. The bad guys will run and try to get away, and sometimes they ditch evidence so that if we do catch them they stand a chance of lesser charges; they only have to count to 50 while in jail instead of 100 and then they're back out on the street again. There were a few cases where suspects actually wanted to fight but usually the fight is simply an effort to get away. When the fight or flight is finished, the subject usually gives in, just like The Game we played when we were kids, not that many years ago.

But back to the instant case and the sprinter we had just bested: Once we had the suspect in custody and I got my bearings from a street sign, I let everybody know where we were. Then J-Hunt and I retraced the route of the race around the house searching for evidence the runner might have dropped. Lying on the ground in plain sight was a baggie containing the tip of an iceberg of hard (crack cocaine, for the uninitiated). Before touching the evidence I called my partner over and showed him what I had found.

I did not see him throw it, I said to Josh.

Me, either, Josh said.

There was no way either of us could honestly say that we could tell how long the bag of dope had been lying there. We needed this kid to admit that he had thrown it. I know what the reader may be thinking: fingerprint the bag. Good idea. But in the real world fingerprints are hard to find, especially on a plastic bag. And if forensics fingerprinted every bag of dope found in the City of Savannah-- forget all of Chatham County-- let's just say they would be busy from now until the end of Time. So I had to find a tricky solution to the dilemma:

63

You got your back up on you, I asked J-Hunt.

No, said Hunt, who usually carried a small KelTec .380 as a get-off-me gun.

Got your back up on you, I asked Officer Tony McBride, who had just arrived on the scene as backup.

Why?

Just give it to me, I said, and follow my lead.

We returned to the unit where the suspect was cuffed and comfortably seated in the cage, and after advising him of his rights-- which, unlike TV, we did not always do-- the kid agreed to chat.

Look, man, I said, *we got a problem. I don't want to do you foul but I gotta know something. I saw you pitch this, I said, holding up the bag of crack. But I didn't see you throw this, I said, holding up Mac's pistol.*

I thought the kid was going to faint.

Fuck no, the kid said. *That's mine*, he said, nodding at the crack. *But I wasn't fuckin' with no gun.*

You know what? I believe you, I said. *I'm not going to charge you with the gun.*

64

The suspect thanked me and swore on everything that he loved that he was telling the truth. You know, just like when he was a kid a few short years ago.

I gave the gun back to Mac and filled out the arrest and booking sheet. The look on Mac's face: priceless.

The following Friday night J-Hunt and I decided it was high time we stepped up our game. We were assigned to Club Closing Time in the Downtown Precinct with Rufus Brown and Floyd Sawyer. Our prime target: the notorious Frozen Paradise on Broughton Street, where the line to get in wrapped around the block and halfway down Jefferson, and where party-goers who lacked the patience to wait until they got inside scored whatever they needed outside.

Rolling past the queue I spotted a hand-to-hand transaction between three subjects. K-Fraiz stopped the car and the four of us broke out like being released from the starting gate at the Kentucky Derby. Two of the subjects quickly decided that rather than talk to us they would take their chances on us catching them. Challenge accepted. The third remained frozen in paradise; good choice.

J-Hunt and I chased the pair of suspects south on Jefferson toward the parking garage while radioing direction of travel and description. Unlike the eastside, we knew exactly where we were and called out clear directions as we rounded the corner between the courthouse and the old jail. There must have been 100 cops within a 10-block radius at this time. The two suspects headed toward MLK Boulevard where they ran into Officer Randy Veal, much to their dismay.

When Josh and I caught up both subjects were on the ground and Veal was standing over them with his ASP drawn. As soon as Veal saw us approach, he pretended his baton was a fishing rod reeling in his catch and doing a little celebration dance. He had signed off for the night after pulling an 8-hour shift and was working off-duty at the Chevron when he heard my call of the race and realized we were heading straight for him. Veal was a retired Army Sergeant and Gulf War Veteran unafraid of getting his hands dirty and was perfectly capable of ending a situation like this one.

I will never forget the look of sheer delight on his face that he had bagged these two trophies. We cuffed them and waited for a unit with a cage for transport.

As is customary, J-Hunt and I retraced the path of the gauntlet. Hunt said they dropped something but I had not seen it. We found two pistols next to a bush near the courthouse. After placing a Beat officer at that point we continued to Frozen Paradise where we found a Glock lying in the middle of the road. If it had been dropped by our suspects, it had been lying there ten or fifteen minutes. I couldn't believe that no one in this frontier town hadn't picked it up and walked off with it.

Meanwhile, Brown and Sawyer have not had much luck finding out what the third musketeer in line at Frozen was up to this evening so we prod the two runners into admitting ownership of the brace of pistols. Three guns in one bust is my idea of a productive night. I love taking guns off people, especially Downtown, and even more so when people who are up to no good illegally possess them.

There is no accurate way to measure what crimes were prevented by removing guns like this but it is a feeling I haven't gotten any other way.

*   *   *   *   *

It was at this point in The Game when command staff took greater notice of what EXPO was accomplishing in restoring law and order to a town equally devoid of both and in total denial of just how serious of a crime problem it has. Apparently, the historic district was too pretty and the businesses on River Street and Broughton were making too much money for anyone to notice the non-stop traffic in and out of the jail and courthouse. Put it this way: In a town of 140,000 residents, 30 to 40 of them went to jail daily. Do the math. Tell me about crime in Savannah.

Sergeant Capers rode back up for Island Precinct Commander Captain James Hieronymus, an outspoken opponent of EXPO in its formative stages but who changed his mind after he saw the job we were doing and started putting in requests for EXPO intervention in his territory. We spent a lot of time in the Islands Precinct and Captain Hieronymus appreciated the fact that we policed the same way he always had.

Previously, the traditional response to any spike in crime in Savannah had been countered with a Total Focus Operation wherein precinct commanders gave up whatever assets they could spare for a weekend night intensive. The cast typically included the crime suppression units, the K-9 unit, the aviation unit (helicopters), and

67

officers wanting overtime. Target areas with a statistical rise in Part 1 crimes were saturated in an effort to deter it.

Total Focus may have been fun but I never really understood the goal, or at least, the execution. I never got why we took 100 officers from different precincts and sent them into a neighborhood for an hour when that kind of police presence causes everything to stop after the first five minutes. Anyone doing anything wrong is apprehended upon initial contact and the rest of the neighborhood goes on alert; all activity ceases, leaving a mass of manpower in the safest place in town with nothing to do for the next 55 minutes except write up motorists for busted tail lights. And it is at this point in the operation that instead of catching criminals we end up alienating the law-abiding public by fucking up their Friday night.

It made no sense to me then and it makes less sense to me now. After my first Total Focus Operation, I unofficially renamed it Hocus Pocus.

The first Hocus Pocus Operation that EXPO participated in was staged one rainy night in Georgia along Augusta Avenue. I was partnered up with J-Hunt, as usual. By now, we had become synonymous with each other to the point where we had been christened with one of those Hollywood hyphenated names: Grunt, a combination of Grogan and Hunt. We made our way over to Millen Street, perhaps the only street in the 'hood experiencing traffic from well-to-do whites if only because it was home to Luther Vann, a painter of repute who had developed a large and prominent following of art collectors from the other side of town. It was there that we observed a car roll through a stop sign right in front of us and so we got behind him and lit him up.

The driver was a young man in a talkative mood. J-Hunt obliged him while I approached on the passenger side. I could tell by the way he was rambling on that this was going to be more than a stop sign. Sure enough, Hunt puts his hand on the roof of the car and signals me to keep the interview rolling. I whispered into my handset for K-9 and Duke was en route almost instantaneously. Hunt could keep subjects talking for days but in order to keep it legal I grabbed the ticket book and began writing out a citation for the stop sign.

Yeah, I know: it's a not a big charge but how many times has the reader scanned the arrest records published online by the SMN to find a stop sign or no seat belt included among a long list of more serious charges? Chances are the reader will never find a suspect written up for just seatbelt; it is an entry-level citation that often leads to more serious charges, to wit:

I am writing up the stop sign violation on this guy while J-Hunt is continuing the interview just long enough for the K-9 Unit to arrive. Dukarski arrives at the scene with K-9 Nick and Josh invites the driver to get out of his vehicle. One look at Nick and the driver changes demeanor from talkative to silent. Nick walks around the car like he's sniffing out a place to pee and then sits by the door, which is his way of telling Duke that he has picked up the scent of narcotics, giving Duke the green light to search.

Hunt detained the driver while Duke and I were getting ready to search. The suspect is still playing it cool, that is until I open the door to his car and begin searching the interior. The suspect cursed Josh in ways I had never heard before and I was in the Army. Spotting a Checkers bag on the front seat, I look inside to find an order of French fries and crack cocaine, a number two on the Bingo menu.

And that was only the first act of this performance. J-Hunt was in rare form this evening. No sooner than we had turned over the evidence in the traffic stop we were on our way to Cuyler-Brownsville to see what's up, and as we made our way to West 33rd and MLK, J-Hunt made a hard right and put the nose of our car on the nose of a parked vehicle and told me to get the driver. I don't know what the hell he saw but I jumped out and went straight for the driver side door. I knew my partner well enough that he never overreacted and if there wasn't time to explain we moved first and talked about it later. We did not ask questions of each other until everyone and everything was secure. We trusted each other implicitly and there was no need for second-guessing any situation in which we found ourselves.

The driver attempted to exit and his buddy in the back was moving all over the place and reaching under the front seat. I put my light directly in his eyes to distract him but he continued to work feverishly. I secured the driver while J-Hunt grabbed the subject in the back seat. Backup EXPO Units arrived on the scene and we got the occupants situated and under control.

J-Hunt reached under the seat and retrieved a full-framed .357 revolver and placed it on the roof of the car. We found crack cocaine on the suspects and crack under car seats. The gun turned out to be one of 50 that had been stolen from a pawnshop, leading to some good tips which ultimately led to an arrest being made in that case also. Even the Chief responded to the scene. When all was said and done, this case put Josh Hunt on the radar screen for detective.

In March 2006, EXPO was summoned to CNT headquarters on Bull Street as they were preparing to move to a new secret location. The purpose of the meeting was to invite our participation in Operation Fire & Ice, in cooperation with the Bureau of Alcohol, Tobacco, Firearms and Explosives (ATF). The targets lived on Fort Argyle Road near the Methingham County line, where Sergeant Tamargo and Mark Galipeau had been working with the Feds doing undercover buys of guns and dope.

The ATF Agent in charge was a big Italian dude who was tatted with full sleeves to the knuckles named Lou Valoze-- Big Lou, to his friends, of which he had very few and all of them were ATF Agents. He did not look like a cop or act like a cop or even brief like a cop. He explained that SWAT was going to do the take down and then CNT and ATF would clean up the mess and deal with the defendants and evidence afterwards. All Lou wanted us to do was hang on the perimeter in case anyone tried to run.

That was EXPO's reputation in the law enforcement community after only 90 days in operation: if someone tried to run, we caught them.

The target was the worst among multiple suspects and the one with the greatest potential for violence. The take down went down at a cheap motel located on Highway 204 at the exit to I-95. J-Hunt and I were positioned behind the motel. The target showed up at the appointed time and SWAT got the drop on them in the parking lot by deploying a flash bang, a diversionary device designed to distract and confuse whatever plans they had in mind. The officer pulled a pin and tossed the cylinder under the suspect's car setting off a loud bang and flash of light as members of the SWAT team surrounded the car and smashed out all the windows. The suspects were pulled out of the car through the window openings and hogtied.

71

Fuck, I said, after assessing the situation. *These boys don't play.*

Then I noticed that the suspects had pissed themselves. So much for that threat of violence.

Josh said: *Remind me never to piss off the ATF.*

(Note: This event marked the first time that I worked with ATF Special Agent Valoze but not the last. After EXPO broke up, I moved on to a drug task force a year later and joined Operation Statesboro Blues, which was designed by Agent Valoze to rid the town of a menacing drug and violent crime problem. In the process Lou and I became friends and he remains one of the people I trust most in this world. We went through tough times together and his story is the subject of another great book, Storefront: Statesboro Blues.)

Shortly after having received this recognition from the ATF, I noticed the first throat-clearing grumblings in our Unit about who was doing all the work and who was not pulling their weight. While it is true that J-Hunt and I often talked about racking up impressive numbers trying to keep up with Brown and Sawyer, we kept it between us. We never taunted our teammates or belittled their accomplishments. The quality of our arrests spoke for itself. But someone was obviously not happy about what was being accomplished and there was some shit talking going on. When Sergeant Capers tired of the bickering, he decided to pull the numbers and put an end to the dispute.

Numbers don't lie, Sarge said.

So he pulled the numbers. When the results were tabulated, J-Hunt and I were first and second in number of arrests. We were surprised but pleased, if only because we set out to be major contributors in this unit of men we looked up to and respected, and we were doing just that. Brown, Sawyer, Baker, Lewis, Frazier and Mitchell were all top producers and the differences between us was razor thin, thin enough to boast but not too loud or too long.

I remember there being a few long faces among those unnamed above when Sarge read out the results. After the meeting broke up and we were walking out the door to hit the streets, Chris Talley ambled alongside me and said:

You know, Grogan, it's not all about locking people up.

I would like to think that Officer Talley was talking about police work in general, as in we had to take the time to shake hands and talk to little old ladies. But EXPO was all about locking up people and not just any people, the worst of the criminal element.

But I saw no reason to check Officer Talley or embarrass him further. Granted, he was not the best cop I ever worked with and we took different views of the big picture. But I have to give Talley credit: Later in his career he proved he was a finisher when he was the central figure in two officer-involved shootings.

Working with EXPO enabled me to get a clearer view of the big picture. I discovered that if we concentrated on small infractions, like traffic tickets and misdemeanors, we tied ourselves up for 30 to 45 minutes, then turned the evidence over, if any, and spent another half

73

hour writing up the report. By focusing on the small stuff we could eat up an entire 12-hour shift and not have accomplished much. Don't get me wrong: I'm not saying that there is no need to address these issues. I'm only saying that it was not my goal in life to write up a record number of Jaywalking violations and it certainly wasn't EXPO's mandate.

J-Hunt and I often turned away suspended license and other minor offenses when that was all there was to the stop. We found a legal way for the driver to proceed and warned them to cure the defect. I made several solid connections by cutting breaks and gained a truckload of trust when I caught probationers or parolees with minor infractions and cut them loose.

Game respects Game, as we say around the clubhouse.

The street saw what I was about and realized what I was after. That is not to say I did not hem up assholes on petty shit. Sometimes putting a suspect in jail for a crack pipe or pissing in public prevented burglaries or other more serious offenses. Sometimes I let them know there was a line and if all I had was a criminal trespass, they caught it if only so they would know not to cross it.

I did not have to flex for long because I quickly earned a decent reputation for being real. Discretion being the biggest tool at my disposal, I realized that I did not have to lock everybody up for everything. I always went out of my way to be fair and to do what was in the best interests of justice. And I usually took the time to explain to suspects what they had done wrong at the time I arrested them, just so they would understand that it was nothing personal, something which my partners noticed and complimented me on long after I left the department.

Later in my career I developed a strong rapport with people I could have locked up but didn't, realizing that the information they could provide me was far more valuable and help me become far more effective than just racking up arrest stats.

So, yes, as a matter of fact, I do understand that The Game is not all about locking up people.

*   *   *   *   *

I have an old friend from high school that I have always regarded as a friend but as the years passed we went our separate ways. We both went on to higher education but I entered the military and law enforcement and she remained in academia. I have nearly completed my masters degree; she earned a doctorate. We lost touch until the advent of social media. We reconnected, still considering her to be a friend. I noticed her posts about diversity and was impressed with her openness in dealing with the touchy subject of race. And then I saw a post that caused me alarm if only because it revealed a mindset that made me look ahead at the kinds of problems police would face in the future:

"Getting pulled over while doing 80 in a 55 and only receiving a warning = white privilege. Dear Officer, thank you very much for letting me go with a warning. Please give equitable treatment to the people of color you pull over."

Reading her post caused my head to spin. I have worked in Law Enforcement for 15 years and I made an untold number of traffic stops, the majority of which were in predominantly black neighborhoods. But not once have I ever issued any enforcement action based on race.

I speed. I have disobeyed speed limits from the first day I obtained a license to drive and I continue to disregard speed limits on a regular basis. But writing a speeding ticket for me would be as hypocritical as making a DUI arrest.

I became even more alarmed as I read some of the comments that followed my friend's post. My biggest issue was the accusation that race had anything to do with the decision of the officer on how to enforce the law. It was at that point I realized that I was dealing with someone who does not live in the real world, who has no experience in the practical truth, someone who has spent their entire adult life in an academic cocoon, and here she is voicing an opinion on how a police officer should make decisions and exercise discretion.

The thought that there are educated people in our society who actually believe that discretionary decisions are made by officers according to some guideline that white people should receive leniency while minorities have the book thrown at them makes me sick to my soul.

Police officers swear an oath to uphold the law without prejudice and with integrity. The suggestion that enforcement is doled out solely based on race or sex or creed or color or any attractive combination of the foregoing spits in the face of what law enforcement stands for.

Are there officers who disregard that oath? Yes.

Are there officers engaged in unethical practices? Yes.
But they are the exception; they are not the rule.

I violated my oath of office when I drank too much alcohol and tried to operate a vehicle. I broke a law I was sworn to uphold. I did not do it because I think the law does not apply to me. I do not violate traffic laws because I do not think they are important. I do it because I'm human and I make mistakes. Sometimes I exercise poor judgment and I accept the consequences. But to imply that officers base leniency on race disregards and is in complete ignorance of what the oath means to officers and what they stand for. To make the statement that our society favors whites and punishes blacks shows an ignorance of the practical world I policed for more than a dozen years.

Not all police are racist.

It is made to seem that way because racism has become the first excuse and last line of defense for people who have exercised poor judgment and refuse to accept the consequences. What I see play out on social media scares me to death. If this mindset that police are inherently racist continues to be proffered by the mainstream media gone berserk, then very soon now legislatures will handcuff cops and kill the discretion so vital to maintaining order. When that discretion is gone, there will be no more grey areas. Officers will be forced to take action regardless of the situation and instead of issuing warnings will issue citations. Misdemeanors will turn into felonies simply because they meet statutory requirements and the discretion coming down on the side of justice and the well-being of the individual will be lost.

Most importantly, without the discretion to prioritize offenses only criminal activity occurring on surface levels will be addressed and what truly matters, and keeps society safe, will receive no emphasis. This world is not one great big college campus surrounded by ivy-covered walls and while I wish we lived in a world where love is the rule and not the exception and predators do not feed on the weak, I know from firsthand experience-- not a classroom-- what this world is really like.

Chapter Four
Remember the Alamo, Motherfucker

Take it from me: No cop gets any real intelligence on what goes on in the streets from people who are not living in those streets. Without intel, a cop has no true direction in effectively combating crime.

In the aftermath of Sergeant Capers pulling the EXPO arrest numbers, rather than remain embarrassed by their lack of performance, the results actually inspired some of our guys to rededicate themselves to the proposition that we were the departmental meat eaters and we would deliver on the promise to eat our way through violent crime in Savannah. The first teammate that comes to mind when it comes to improvement is Terrance Jackson.

Jack was a retired sergeant first class and a Gulf War Army Veteran but that alone fails to describe him accurately, if only because there are no words, really. However, I will try:

Jack was the kind of guy that if you told him to take down a tree he would find a way despite any and all obstacles. But if you had him look at a forest and pick out the tree that had to go, you would be waiting for a long, long time.

Before EXPO, He was assigned to afternoon shift in Central Precinct and was tasked with training rookies despite the fact that public speaking was not Jack's strong suit. He had a distinct speech pattern punctuated with um and uh instead of commas. Four months into our operation um Jack had assumed the evidence role. He took the kit Powell put together uh and helped the rest of us, you see, speed up our cases by handling the evidence so we could, uh, get back on the street and find more shit.

When Capers pulled our arrest numbers and Jack came up on the shorter side, his response was classic Jack: he did not utter a single syllable, not so much an um or an uh, but sat with his arms folded and his tongue pushing out his cheek, and the only sound coming from him was the creak of his leather gun belt when he shifted in his seat that sounded like a fart.

The next few days, however, were The Terrance Jackson Show. He made 5 felony arrests in two days. One of his busts was staged at the world infamous Alamo Plaza, a motor lodge that old folks in Savannah remember when they were kids and forbidden to darken its portals as adults. It was designed to remotely resemble the historic site in Texas where the famous battle was fought during the Revolution in 1836, when 100 brave cowboys under the direction of Davy Crockett, Jim Bowie and William Travis held off the entire Mexican Army for two assaults but not the third. "Remember the Alamo" became the war cry of those soldiers who later attacked and defeated Santa Anna.

But in Savannah 100 years later, the Alamo Plaza was remembered only by young men who were looking for cheap hookers and had been largely forgotten ever since, except by men one step above homeless and in need of dime bags and dime pieces in decline.

In a town celebrated for its historic district, the Alamo Plaza has a sense of history all its own. Granted, it is far away from the house museums facing Savannah's squares, but if these walls could talk, oh what stories they could tell. In a town forested by historic plaques, maybe the State of Georgia should erect one in front of the Alamo Plaza, where generations of Savannah boys became men in a matter of minutes and for only twenty bucks.

The Alamo Plaza in 2006 was a honey hole of street level drug activity. If we did not come out of there with at least one arrest, we were just plain off our game. As soon as we cleared the front gate people scurried in every direction. All except Anthony Bell, who lived peaceably in the last room as you exit the complex and was the friendliest guy you could ever meet. Every time we dropped in on the Alamo, Mister Bell would be sitting outside the door to his room with his buddy "One-eye". He was quick to greet us and saved us all the trouble of having to look around by filling us in on all the latest comings and goings:

Man, I think the girl in 217 is sellin' pussy or *Man, the guy in 371 is slingin' rock.*

Sometimes his tips panned out, sometimes not, but he was always in a cheerful and talkative mood. He even went so far as to invite us inside his room to look around, just to make sure we knew that he was clean.

This day though, old "One-eye" was leaning against the wall and while we were speaking to some other residents, I heard Jack say *Hey, what you doin?* I turned and saw "One-eye" standing back up and held his hands out to say *I ain't got nothing.* Jack walked right up to him and bent over to a rock that was on the ground. Jack moved it and found a different kind of rock in a plastic baggie underneath. Jack grabbed ol'

"One-eye" and put him in cuffs. Of course, "One-eye" objected saying we hadn't caught him with anything but old Jack had seen him slowly and very uncomfortably slide down the wall and move the rock and then slide back up the wall. Of course, Mr. Bell was in shock that crack could be found so close to his apartment and was visibly upset with his friend for that type of behavior. Good Ol' Jack and the cast of characters at the Alamo.

Jack could turn it on and off at will, this ability of his to make it happen, even if he preferred playing a supporting role handling evidence. I learned a lot from Jack. Hell of a street cop. I continued to work with him long after EXPO and enjoyed every second of it.

If J-Hunt and I were patrolling the Downtown Precinct, we headed to the river when it was time for meal break and dropped in on our old friend Nick at the Olympia Cafe. Nick and his people always took good care of the thin blue line getting fatter at his table. We were always treated royally and there was nothing on his menu of Greek delicacies that I did not crave. Just as we tucked into dinner on one particular occasion, the tones went out: Signal 7 (Shooting), Montgomery and Lorch.

The location was well known to anyone who worked the Downtown Precinct, especially J-Hunt. This was Sharron's Lounge, owned by the Scott family, who were some of the nicest folks in town. Their son Big Daddy, however, was no stranger to us. Despite his scrapes with the law, Big Daddy had a mutual understanding with and a respect for J-Hunt.

82

We jumped up and headed out to see what was going down at Sharron's Lounge.

Hunt drove so I did not have to hear about going the wrong way.

Up the ramp, down Bay Street, and straight up MLK, we were on the lookout for a male suspect running toward Kayton Homes in a blue striped shirt. Several units had responded to the call ahead of us. We turned onto Mo Brown and made the first right onto Draper, when I looked through the window of a car parked on the southside of the street and saw a young man in the passenger side pulling off a blue striped shirt like he was in a hurry to get laid in the back seat. His eyes were as big as softballs when he saw us. Hunt had seen him too; our car came to a halt. I jumped out and ran toward the suspect as he bailed out of his car and took off. We called out the chase over the radio and I saw Joe Groover hauling ass down Mo Brown straight for the suspect. With Officer Groover was his trusty K-9 partner, Nero.

I had seen canine officers sniff out dope tons of times but I had never seen a K-9 deployed on a take down and I knew I was about to witness my first. The suspect broke hard to the right and Groover released Nero after telling the man to stop.

It may interest the reader to know that when a K-9 is released, all Law Enforcement officers in the vicinity are advised to freeze so that the dog is not distracted. But it is also important to add that adrenaline is a hell of a drug and stopping is not something that comes naturally to me while in pursuit of a suspect.

The Emperor Nero was closing in on his prey and it was everything I imagined it to be: a sleek, athletic animal running full throttle, eye on the prize. The suspect suddenly changed course and ran up a flight of stairs to an apartment building. Nero was faked out by the move and shot past the stairway. I reengaged and headed for the stairs just as the suspect was coming back down. Then I heard Groover yell, *STOP*! I froze in place. And then I saw Nero, who had circled back and was under the staircase, with a look on his face like *I Got You Now, Muthafucker*, and made contact with his prize.

The impact that this animal made with the suspect was no less impressive than a linebacker hitting a running back head-on in the backfield. 10-95 after a couple of bites, then Groover commanded Nero to release when the struggle was gone. Once Nero was secured, we placed the suspect in cuffs.

I stepped back, looked around and found a large ziploc bag containing several smaller clear plastic baggies filled with marijuana but no gun. We searched the suspect, searched the car, but no gun. We turned over the suspect to detectives and later discovered he was not the shooter we were looking for nor did he have any connection to the shooting at Sharron's Lounge. We had gone looking for a shooter in a blue striped shirt and found someone identical to the description but guilty of a different crime.

I cannot tell the reader how many times this happens: we set out to find a 9-foot redheaded giant with one leg only to discover there are two of them in the same vicinity and both are up to no good.

On a day when J-Hunt was in court and I was paired up with K-Fraiz, I instinctively knew I was in for an eventful afternoon.

Kelvin came to EXPO from the Islands Precinct, a former Savannah State defensive lineman who sent the needle of the big scale in the lobby of Publix straight to 300, his mere presence made even the most aggressive suspect think twice-- hell, think 300 times-- about physical resistance. Captain Heironymus had not been pleased to let Frazier go to EXPO and was not shy about letting people know it, either. But K-Fraiz quickly established himself as a go-to guy when it was time to get It and go, and there was no doubt that this is where he was supposed to be in the law enforcement world.

We were over near Westlake in an unmarked car but still clad in our highly visible Yellow Shirts. Under these circumstances, the unmarked car was going to get us about a half block closer to suspects before they realized who we were.

We turned onto Koneman and saw a young man climbing out of a green Dodge Ram. He looked around and got a fix on us. EXPO had been around long enough for this guy to know if a big black dude and a little white fucker in bright yellow shirts are riding around together it can only mean one thing, POLICE. Without missing a beat the subject closes the door to the truck and jumps into a waiting green Pontiac idling nearby and they take off like a rocket.

I jumped out to look around the truck while K-Fraiz kept his eye on the Pontiac. I called in the tag of the truck and dispatch came right back with a description of a different vehicle. I'm standing next to the truck and could hear music playing from inside and knew one of two things had happened: either the engine had been left running or there was an electrical issue that occurs when steering columns are spiked.

After a delay, other EXPO units called out that they were out with the Pontiac in the driveway of a residence around the corner. I made my way there and spoke to the driver who, for some reason that he did not want to share, had twelve grand in cash in his pocket and told me that he really didn't know the passenger who had jumped in his car back there next to the truck. The story went downhill from there. I mean, it was a weak story and nobody with twelve large falls under the category of mentally challenged.

We got a call to return to the Dodge Ram, where Floyd pointed out that there was a joint going to waste in the ashtray and it was possible to get a contact high if you stood too close to the truck. We searched it and found a sack of seeds and a Tech 9 machine pistol fully loaded and wrapped in a towel behind the driver's seat. All of the evidence added up to an interesting scenario. But before I could begin the field interview or advise the suspect of his rights, he started interviewing me and asking all kinds of questions about what I had found in the truck.

Look man, he said, *I know you found that Tech 9. It's registered*...he would later mention he had been locked up for robbery before, and, uh, you know.

As a fact of business, I happened to know that a felon in possession of a firearm is strictly a no-no. I called Sarge and he made all of the notifications and in the next few minutes task force officers from the DEA and ATF responded to the scene. The DEA did not show up because of the drugs; they showed up because of the money. Anytime a suspect is holding ten grand or more in cash and narcotics are present, the DEA wants to know if they are connected. There were five of us standing there counting out the currency on the hood of our unit like it was some sort of floating crap game.

As time went by I also remembered this episode as the beginning of a long and fruitful relationship with Daryl McCormick and the Savannah Field Office of the ATF.

When J-Hunt returned to work from court we took up where we had left off in West Savannah, running along the railroad tracks alongside Comer Street. We were tailing Frazier and Lewis at patrol speed in search of activity. One of the craftier ways we cultivated in speaking with subjects involved parking violations. We often stopped and spoke to drivers who were parked facing against traffic, a minor violation, but reason enough to stop and talk. If we found no other infraction, we told them to park their vehicle properly and were on our way. Most of the time, however, this simple infraction transitioned into something bigger.

Spotting a car on Comer facing south on the northbound side of the street, two men were sitting inside and both of them reached under their seats when they saw us approach. We advised them that we had stopped because of the way they were parked but looking inside I spotted two sacks of cocaine, one under each seat. The driver said he didn't know nuthin' about nuthin but his passenger was more forthcoming.

Hell yeah, that's mine, he said, pointing to the larger of the two bags. *But that other shit ain't. And fuck it,* he added, *I ain't the only one going down for this shit. That shit is his,* he said, pointing at the smaller bag. And then he added: *I knew I shouldn't have come out tonight with this black cloud bad luck havin' muthafucka.*

* * * * *

EXPO may not have lasted very long-- eleven months, to be exact-- but lasted long enough for us to get to know certain neighborhoods. We were up and down Augusta Avenue and in and out of Cuyler-Brownsville, Westlake Apartments and Hazzard County so often that we knew who was who, who hung with whom, and who called the shots in each vicinity. More importantly, the shot callers knew us and they knew we weren't driving by to say hello or stopping to shake hands and kiss babies. EXPO got to be known for business. We were the Other Half of The Game.

To the average person in Savannah, the streets appear to be run by a bunch of animals running wild; that is not so. Everything is connected and every action has an equal reaction. There are rules to The Game and a general consensus on how it is played. Respect has a lot to do with how far a situation will escalate and how much information gets shared. It is true between criminals and it is also true between criminals and cops. Maybe the relationships seem unsophisticated on the surface but there is a constant sizing up that goes on between officers and citizens, and even more so by criminals encountering police.

The Yellow Shirts established a hard but fair reputation during our brief existence. It was known on the street that if EXPO had a reason to stop, the stop happened. But if the subject wasn't wanted and wasn't up to anything, the subject would be on his way shortly. There was also the understanding that if a suspect was up to no good, the suspect would be dealt with. And there was no question that if a suspect ran or tried to fight, he was guaranteed to lose. Unwritten rules, but after we became known in the 'hood where The Game is real, both sides understood and respected what the other side was doing.

Not all guys standing on the corner are evil people. They are doing what they do and doing it the best way they know how. A subject once explained: The light man don't give a fuck if you have a degree or not , he only understands money, and a hungry baby don't give a fuck where its food comes from, either.

This was the kind of lesson I learned on the streets of these poor neighborhoods in Savannah, and will never forget.

The nature of The Game has always been that it is the suspect's job to try and get away and it is my job to catch them. If they get away, I can't be mad at them and if I catch them, they can't be mad at me. That's The Game. If you play, there are rules. While I do not agree with many of the choices made by these individuals, I admit a grudging respect for the way they stand up for what they do and who they are. I have been frustrated so many times in my career by subjects who have street logic so ingrained in them that they won't speak to police even when it benefits them or brings justice for a family member. But I know they distrust police and I respect that they stand for what they believe, even if it's deadly.

I have served in combat in Baghdad and Savannah, and both places have one thing in common: men who do not waiver from their beliefs. I always treated everyone on the streets of both places with respect and I expected the same in return. I did not always get it, that's just how it goes.

89

Sergeant Capers had a way of putting the situation into perspective, saying: *We start out here* (holding his hand flat, palm down, at his waist) *but if they go here* (raising hand to eye level), *we go with them.*

Capers expected us to be professional at all times but he never expected us to be pussies. Law enforcement today trains officers to be "firm but flexible". While I have always allowed citizens to vent and speak their peace, I have limits, and depending on the lack of peacefulness that limit is much less. I also have a low tolerance for stupid. That said, I usually got respect because I always gave it. The bad guys knew me and I knew them. They knew I was fair but I had been tried enough times to establish that I gave as good as I got, and then some.

At one point, Josh and I had more uses of force between the two of us than the entire department combined. That is not to say that all we did was bust heads. But we stuck our noses in situations where the consequences for our opponents was severe enough that they could not let it ride. The reader will have to trust me when I say that when coming up against me and Josh or Rufus and Floyd or Lew and Frazier, ten times out of nine the suspect would elect to fight me and Josh first. It would not end well for the suspect, but he would try it.

Midway through the mission, I think Capers was still wondering about me and Hunt. We were racking up more arrests than any other duo in the Unit and he could not figure it out. After all, we were white boys from someplace else patrolling a black inner city and Yankees, to boot. We did not have half the familiarity of our precincts that the majority of homegrown talent on the team possessed and we were half the size of the starters.

J-Hunt and I were walking out of roll call one afternoon when Sarge called us over. *Hey*, he said, *I got one for you two.* Then he handed me a booking photo of a guy wanted for armed robbery. The only thing anybody knew about this guy was that he had a twin brother living on the southside. Neither Hunt nor I had any clue where we were on the southside but, hey, we were always up for a challenge.

We left the lot and pulled into the address of the apartment complex and within 60 seconds had the suspect in custody. Being one of two people who looked exactly the same in a town where we were always grabbing the wrong one, he tried to convince us that we had the wrong one.

I'm the good son, he said. *You're lookin' for my brother.*

Okay, Josh said. *We will hold onto you and go find your brother. We will arrest him and put him in jail, and tell him you ratted him out.*

Okay, he said. *You got me.*

I called Sarge with the 10-95.

Bingo, Sarge, I said.

Who? You got who?

The guy wanted for armed robbery, I said. *The twin.*

91

But you only been gone ten minutes, Sarge said.

Has it been that long?

I didn't think we'd been gone that long, I said.

You motherfuckers, Sarge said.

I think he meant that as a compliment.

*   *   *   *   *

By April, EXPO lost Josh Hunt to the detective's office and I was all alone in this world. It was bound to happen sooner or later. It's what he wanted and the promotion was a good move for a man on the move career-wise.

Now here's the thing about Capers: Hunt was his big numbers guy, the leader in arrests and solid arrests, at that. Hunt had established himself as one of the leaders of the department in general and EXPO in particular. One call from Capers to the Chief reminding him of his promise could have blocked this move and kept Hunt where he was needed but Capers did not believe in that. By blocking Hunt's promotion Capers would have been guilty of the very thing he had protested when he was forming the Unit, that Supervisors raise hell when their precinct is raided of the best talent, and it would not have helped Hunt at all. Hunt had proven he had the skill, knowledge and ability to police and a move to Detectives would allow him to learn more, and that is exactly what he did.

Now here's the thing about Josh Hunt: J-Hunt did not disappoint. He spent a short amount of time sorting out property crimes before moving to homicide where he killed it (pun intended). Homicide is where Josh always wanted to be, where he belonged and when he got there he solved every single case he was assigned for the next seven years and even a few cold cases when he had nothing else to do.

The only other detective in Savannah police history to accomplish this feat was Andre Oliver-- and the reader of this book never read about this in the *Savannah Morning News*.

It took me awhile to get used to riding without J-Hunt. After all, we spent more time together during our 4-month partnership than Josh spent alone with his wife in ten years.

Go back and read that last sentence again. It is not exaggeration.

It was like Batman losing Robin (and after he reads this we will forever argue about who was Batman). We knew what each other was thinking to the point where we had a natural rhythm. We were in total sync, like Lennon and McCartney. J-Hunt put the punch in Grunt and was the better reason why our team was number one in the friendly competition that made EXPO the run-and-gun special op that it was. And yet if you asked him, Josh would tell you that Rufus Brown was team captain and the best cop there ever was-- a legend-- and I loved him for it. Josh would also say for years after he was long gone from SCMPD that his days on EXPO were the most fun he ever had in a uniform even though it was twelve to fourteen hours a day, five and six days a week, if only because the job pushed him to improve.

However, I also had the distinct impression that the other teams on EXPO had the mistaken impression that J-Hunt was doing all the work of our team and that I was just along for the ride; I was Robin. Maybe it was just my way of putting pressure on myself. Even before EXPO I pushed myself. Nothing was good enough and no matter how well I performed I knew I could always do better. I credit my success in life to this line of thought but it came at a dear price in causing me a lot of stress.

After EXPO had been in existence for six months we had established a list of contacts that kept us up to date on what was going on in the street and the location of wanted suspects. Nineteen-year-old Christopher Middleton had been gunned down in Cuyler-Brownsville, in a dispute over drug territory. Homicide Detectives identified Antonio Mitchell aka Truckhead as the shooter and obtained a murder warrant for his arrest. But they had a hard time turning up Truckhead and so they put in a call to Sergeant Capers and asked him to sic EXPO on their suspect.

Capers had a novel of way of issuing the challenge to his crew: As soon as Truckhead is in custody, he said to us, you can have the rest of the night off.

Sawyer and Brown had contacts all over Savannah in general and CBV in particular. Nothing moved from MLK to Ogeechee Road and from West Victory to West Anderson without Floyd and Rufus catching wind of it. Floyd stopped the first person he saw on his estimable list of contacts and told him we were looking for Truckhead. The contact nodded and kept walking, then stopped dead in his tracks when Floyd called over his shoulder: This neighborhood is shut down until we have Truck.

94

It took less than five minutes for Floyd to receive the anonymous tip that Truckhead was en route to Mickey D's at Victory and Montgomery.

Young and Mitchell were the first to get there and without incident, scooped up a murder suspect and achieving Bingo.

We called Sarge and let him know, he's 10-95.

Bingo, Sarge, said Mitchell.

Who? You got who?

Truckhead, said Mitchell.

Damn, y'all boys are something else, replied Capers.

Unfortunately, we did not get the next eleven hours and fifty minutes off. Savannah was far too busy for that luxury. Hell, we didn't want it anyway. But it was a huge boost to morale to be able to deliver in this fashion whenever a challenge was issued. And the boys in Homicide were growing accustomed to our ability to get shit done.

EXPO got a reputation in the street and when the Yellow Shirts entered neighborhoods, word got around quick. These guys knew if there was one Yellow Shirt, several were not far away. We had to adapt because once they saw one of us, there was no more sneaking up on people.

95

Sergeant Capers had the solution to our problem: he turned a paddy wagon into a Trojan horse. One day, Sarge decided we would load up in "The Cruiser". Each precinct had a van that was used to transport prisoners to jail. The back had no windows and long benches to accommodate multiple offenders. Cruisers were traditionally driven by older officers who would rather transport other people's messes than have to generate their own paperwork. In Downtown and Central Precincts, one could eat up a whole shift doing nothing but transporting other officer's arrests. The boys on the corners didn't think anything of the Cruiser when it rolled past.

Sergeant Capers, being a man of letters, adapted his own version of the Trojan Horse by loading a SCMPD paddy wagon with eight members of EXPO, sliding past sentries who had become accustomed to seeing the Cruiser with some older corporal behind the wheel drive by on its way someplace else. Capers had us load up in the back and we had to hold the doors because, being a transport van, it locked from the outside.

Sarge pulled down Waters Avenue and drove to the corner of East Duffy Street, always known for a decent amount of drug activity and the unsuspecting players, as usual thought nothing of it, that is until.......We bust out of the back door and scattered in eight different directions. Guys ran in every direction. Some got farther than others but most just ran because they were in shock. I remember one young man ran in circles screaming as loud as he could, clutching his head. He ran as fast as he could but stayed in a tight circle and went nowhere. I don't think he even knew why he was running other than he was in shock. To this day, Capers is still proud of the innovation.

It was no surprise that EXPO became the go-to for detectives. If they were working cases and in need of information, we made contact with those in the know or found whom detectives wanted to talk to. We recovered a warehouse filled with stolen property that enabled property crimes to close cases. The notorious Big Tom's burglary was solved when EXPO turned up the weapons that were involved. We got a lot of guns and the people who illegally possessed them and we piled up a mountain of dope.

Chapter Five
Smell the Gun, Leave the Croissan'wich
(with apologies to Peter Clemenza)

Since 1994, the Chatham County Counter Narcotics Team (CNT) has been tasked with mid-level narcotics investigations; more than a dime bag, less than Tony Montana. CNT is made up of officers from Savannah-Chatham, Chatham County Sheriff's Office, Tybee Island, Pooler and other small municipalities in Chatham County. CNT is well funded and in possession of all the high tech gadgetry any outfit could want and every kid wants for Christmas.

However, I had a bad taste in my mouth for CNT and their particular brand of bullshit, stemming from the following encounter:

Hitch Village was home to some of the baddest drug dealers in Savannah since Ricky Jivens. I had racked up a lot of experience while riding Hitch, and in my spare time sat around my kitchen table at night putting together an illustrated crime family tree, just for fun. Can't tell the players without a program and I have always been very visual when it comes to my memory.

I remember that fateful day when J-Hunt called out that he was chasing two guys who were heading towards Anderson Lane near Lincoln. I got in the area as fast as I could and a few minutes later I spotted two guys fitting Hunt's description, one of them had a low haircut and I remember thinking the other one had a "poufy" fro. I asked J Hunt to describe their hair and he said one of them has "poufy" hair. I stopped them and when I asked them to approach my car, one took off running, or tried to anyway. I remember grabbing a hold of one while the other attempted to fly. It was kind of comical because he was so slow, I couldn't tell if he was joking or if he was actually trying to get away. I held onto my guy and called out the other was "running" north on Lincoln. Luckily, John Nevin was just around the corner and cut off the runner at the pass, who just happened to be in possession of an ounce of crack.

The subject I held onto was holding seven thousand dollars, cash money. His partner had an ounce of hard. By the time the dust settled and Hunt advised these were not the guys he was chasing (again, funny how that works out), There were enough supervisors in the area and they decided to call CNT. The ensuing investigation led to the recovery of another eighteen grand, which required that I make a trip to CNT headquarters on Bull Street after booking the suspects. And that is when something happened that still blows my mind to this day:

The CNT agent scratched my name off of the arrest/booking sheet and put his in its place. Noticing my puzzlement and dismay, the agent made a point of explaining that this is the way things were done around CNT but that I would be credited with the assist.

Now I have to say that I've never been a big numbers guy, especially at this point in my illustrious career. I did not receive a bonus for number of arrests or the amount of dope I recovered or for confiscated weapons, so numbers never meant much other than acting as a gauge to see where I stood among my peers. But there was a principle at stake here: I made the stop, Nevin does the running, the CNT gains entrance for us to the suspect's apartment because the suspect is on probation, and then the CNT guy scratches off my name and takes the credit? Have I got that right?

I never had violent crimes or robbery detectives scratch my name off of an arrest sheet when I caught one of their bad guys. I thought what the CNT Agent did was low-class then and I'm of the same opinion now.

Thereafter, I made it a point that whenever I had a warrant to serve I made sure that the officer who located the suspect got the credit for the arrest.

Then again, department policy was unclear to me whether the recovery of a certain amount of drugs required a call to CNT or that they were to be called only in the event of meeting a specified weight or threshold. All I knew was I did not want to deal with CNT and neither did anyone else on EXPO.

We were hauling marijuana by the pound and crack by the ounce and cocaine by the ounce plus a bunch of guns, providing us the kind of leverage on suspects that could be utilized to gain intelligence. If EXPO had a downfall, it's that we did not know what to do with all the intel we gleaned from these arrests. SCMPD did not collect and share intel, a major flaw that persists as of this writing.

Four years later I was able to still make good on intelligence that I had personally stored away from my EXPO days when Sergeant Capers and I reunited with the ATF for the SARGE campaign.

EXPO made a large number of drug busts during Total Focus Operations that CNT was supposed to be making. When CNT showed up after the fact and tried to hijack the arrests, Sergeant Capers would give them the hand; the rest of us gave them the finger. Having been repeatedly disrespected by CNT to the point of being burned, it created an uncooperative atmosphere between Units. And the larger problem, again, was that vital information went unshared. If nothing else, that seems to be one of the few drawbacks when stubborn alpha males are forced to play in the same cesspool.

I recall the night when I backed up Judd West and Jeff Graff when they caught a dude with compressed cocaine the size of a softball. There had been a fight over it, but when West was one of the combatants it never played out well for his competition. Officer West was a fireplug and an angry one, at that. He called CNT to adopt the case.

Watch out for CNT, I warned him. *Watch the way they handle it.*

I told him about my incident and how they had scratched my name off the A&B and he chuckled.

They ain't gonna do that to me, West vowed.

And then I volunteered to transport the suspect and hang around long enough to peep the arrest/booking sheet; same thing. Same damn thing.

The hostility between EXPO and CNT and the lack of cooperation got so bad that Lieutenant Mitchell called Sergeant Capers and invited us to CNT headquarters for a sit-down. Mitchell was a good guy that meant well but I don't think he understood the true nature of the problem and the amount of bad blood that had built up if all he ever heard was CNT's side of the story. We made every effort to maintain our collective professional composure while explaining to Mitchell how agents who worked for him picked which cases they deigned to help us with.

101

After we had gone on for twenty minutes running down his crew, I observed that Lieutenant Mitchell wore the countenance of a man who had been made to look bad: he had the funding, the fleet, the firepower, and the informant base...but EXPO was making all the big street level cases and hitting targets that were attractive. And when we were finally finished making our case against CNT, the lieutenant gave us the We're All On The Same Team speech. I disagreed with him then and for all the rest of my days with SCMPD.

After I had returned to B Watch and EXPO was over, I got a call from Sergeant Tamargo, who was working as a liaison for Major Regan in Special Ops. He wanted to know if I had anything on the Hitch Village Posse. I rambled on about the Ferguson family enterprise and connected the mothers and brothers and cousins, and then Tamargo cut me off.

Hey, he said, *put something together on them for me.*

So I polished off my PowerPoint presentation that I had been working on in my spare time, linking the Ferguson brothers to their network based on the intel I had been gathering. I had a contact that was not exactly an informant but would point out certain people and things at advantageous times. Tamargo could tell I had a good hold on what was going on in Hitch, so he asked me to do him a solid and introduce my contact to CNT.

I threw up a little in my mouth at the suggestion, and then told Tamargo that I would talk to the kid to see if he would be willing to talk to anybody else. As luck would have it, I stopped my guy a day later holding a little weed. I hit him up and asked if he would talk to CNT,

Hell no, he said. *CNT gets people killed.*

102

That's what he said to me and I have never forgotten it.

I'm no snitch, he said. *But I'll let you know as much as I can.*

I went back to Tamargo with his response. The best I could do under these circumstances, I told him, was to relay questions and answers between them.

The next day I am walking around Fred Wessels with Star Corporal Holmes, who was assigned as the Public Housing Enforcement Officer, and made inquiry into who resided in a certain apartment. Holmes got a defensive look on his face and told me to back off because there was an upcoming operation and I shouldn't get in the way. He implied that CNT and the Feds were doing something big and it was way over my head.

Just so happens, as we were on our walk, we spotted two young men that I knew standing at the bottom of the stairs on the backside of the building. I grabbed a young man I knew as "Hot Boy Roy" and I went through my usual routine, patted him down and found what I was looking for. I knew "Hot Boy Roy" from several encounters, a few that made me run all the way across the projects to catch him. I tried to be cool but Holmes had seen me pull something out of the kid's pocket and wanted to know what it was. I played it off like it was nothing and the kid played along, knowing I'm trying to front for him, but Holmes persisted.

Holmes was rarely involved in arrests and did not want to let this opportunity pass him by. So I had to take the kid to the precinct and Holmes excitedly put in a call to CNT. The kid looked me squarely in the eye and told me he could help me if I could get him a low bond.

103

I don't want this to cost my mama a lot of money, he said.

I got you, I said.

CNT decided to take this case, not because of the size of the haul, which was miniscule, but because of their interest in the targeted apartment. I was a beat cop with zero clout as far as getting bonds reduced; CNT agents did it all the time. I told the CNT agent I could flip a valuable informant in exchange for a reduced bond and the agent agreed to the deal. But when we showed up for the kid's first appearance in court, the agent was a no-show and the kid got no help with the bond that ended up costing his mama plenty.

Listen: I was effective in Hitch Village because everyone knew my word meant something. If I said it, I meant it. I had told this kid I would get him help on his bond and CNT fucked us both.

I worked near and around CNT often over the next few years. Imagine how I felt on the day I received temporary marching orders assigning me to CNT for Operation Raging Waters. Rather than hold the reader in suspense, I will say from the jump that as long as I was connected to CNT I got nothing accomplished. It was only when Sergeant Rusty Smith and Agent Gene Harley decided that they were no longer interested in the operation that I was picked up by Sergeant Oglesby from Tactical Response and Prevention (TRAP) and I was able to make any advances that helped the operation. I learned more in one week from Oglesby about working informants and search warrants than I would learn in more than 200 hours of training and three years in the field with a narcotics task force.

CNT was the single most uncomfortable assignment I ever pulled and I thank God it was temporary. Sergeant O gave me a new set of tools to play with and I put them to good use. But I will be damned if CNT didn't turn up at the tail end of Operation Raging Waters and try to take credit for the work that had been done entirely by Josh Hunt and TRAP.

And now you know why-- well, most of the reasons-- I hate CNT.

To be fair, a lot of good officers have been assigned to CNT and done good things while they were there. I have joked with my friends who get picked up by CNT that I will enjoy their friendship again once they have completed their assignment. John Nevin, Mike Arango, Dave Arbizo and Chase Cogswell went over to them and worked big cases and did good things for Chatham County. CNT is still in operation today and I read big news about the Unit. The only encouragement I have for its future is that CNT is now run by Everett Regan, a retired Major from Metro and SPD. Regan is a bulldog and a true cop and had the good sense to bring guys like George Gundich to help him out.

*   *   *   *   *

In June, 2006 we had a Black Shirt Day during which we crept around the Edgemere/Sackville side of town. Brown was first to move in on three guys acting in a suspicious manner while standing around a parked truck. When I had enough backup in place I approached the vehicle and went through my routine. The driver did not want me anywhere near his truck. When I looked inside I saw why: Underneath the armrest was a large plastic bag containing several smaller bags of marijuana. I cuffed the driver and searched the truck and landed on his bomb: two Lay's potato chip cans packed to the brim with bags of weed, powder and crack. Bingo!

The bad part of this story did not develop until several months later when I was called to testify in a suppression hearing on this case. I made the mistake of testifying on memory without reviewing my report. During examination I left out a few key details and all of the evidence was thrown out. It was the right call by the Judge and a valuable lesson in preparedness for court. A solid, slam-dunk case wasted because I failed to prepare. I made a personal vow that it would never happen again.

K-Fraiz and I paired up for a while. We made a string of good arrests while riding together but what I remember most was the time we went to Clinch and Stark, a honey hole for street level drug deals. At ground zero I spotted a car with three subjects inside.

Now depending on the severity of the offense and the experience of the offender, I have found that police get three types of looks: The first look happens when there is a minor infraction and the offender is relatively savvy, and then we get a quick glance and look away as though they have not noticed the police; the second look comes from inexperienced offenders who are committing a serious offense, and then we get a wide-eyed stare that is unable to look away; and the third look comes from experienced offenders who won't look at police regardless of the seriousness of the offense, and then all we get is them tracking every move we make peripherally. The subjects in question were just leaving the "studio" and as we passed they all looked at us with wide eyes. I knew we were onto something good so we turned around.

The driver stayed cool, obeying the speed limit, stopping at signs, and using directional signals. Basically, he did nothing wrong. K-Fraiz and I discussed all the reasons for a stop and could not come up with a legal reason to stop these subjects. Then I noticed there was no rearview mirror on the windshield. Both doors had mirrors, but did they meet the legal standard? I did not know and neither did Frazier. We followed the subjects for several blocks without finding a reason to stop them so we let them go. We turned off. Every sense in my body said these guys were sitting on a bomb but we will never know. That's The Game. If you don't have it, cut it loose. Even if we knew in our bones they were dirty.

EXPO has been accused over the years of making bad stops and bad arrests but I am here to tell the reader that was not the case. We kept each other honest.

The longer EXPO went, the more competitive we got, a dynamic that made us better at our job but made for hardheadedness as well. On a night I was riding with Mitchell along Richards Street in West Savannah, I noticed the interior light inside of a vehicle parked the wrong way. I pulled alongside and we exited our unit and approached the vehicle just as the driver opened his door. He was freakin' huge and so I stopped him from getting out. The unmistakable sweet stench of stinkweed billowed out of his ride and the driver struggled to get out. I put my hand on his shoulder to prevent him from running or taking a swing at me, and then advised him that the only reason we stopped was to tell him he was parked in the wrong direction. He had blown his high and was trying to get to his feet. I preferred that he remain seated with both hands in plain view.

Relax, I told him. *If all we have here is a parking violation, you'll be fine.*

He was not fine and he did not appear to be reassured.

107

Look, man, I said, *if you're worried about not having a license, chill out because you were not operating the vehicle.*

He dropped his shoulders and relaxed, just as Mitchell appeared behind me and over my shoulder. I tapped Mitchell and motioned for him to cover the passenger side where another subject was seated. Mitchell wasn't concerned about the passenger and pointed out to the driver that he could smell weed.

Well that did it: the door swung open and this big dude pops out like a 300-pound jack-in-the-box. All I could think about while we were tag-teaming this guy was if the passenger has a gun, we are both dead. But the passenger was stoned to the point of paralysis and did not so much as flinch, fart or flip a bird.

We cuffed the big fella and I told Mitchell to grab the passenger. Instead, Mitchell hopped into the driver's seat and began searching the car. Jeff Graff and his partner showed up in support and secured the passenger still lost in a purple haze. Mitchell pops out, obviously excited by the crack he has found, and says to me: *Grogan, you know who's arrest this is.*

I could not have given a shit who's arrest this was. I laid into Mitchell for leaving a suspect unsecured but he was too happy to hear me. This is my arrest, Mitchell said, and it was all I could take. I lunged at him. Graff grabbed me and pushed me away.

I don't think I've ever been so mad at a fellow officer that I wanted to fight but I was that night. And to this day I don't think Mitchell is aware. I will say it again: Mitchell had terrific instincts for sourcing trouble but he had no idea as to the big picture.

As with every other member of EXPO, I had a competitive relationship with Mitchell. I remember one night we were breaking bread at Hardee's on Ogeechee, talking shit when the topic of foot speed came up. Mitchell claims he is the fastest thing on two feet since Maurice Greene and the rest of the shift is laughing at him in response. Mitchell takes exception, as alpha males will do, and checks me: *Grogan, I'd smoke yer ass.*

Now I have never claimed to be the world's fastest man but over short distances I can hold my own and some of yours. Mitchell kept up the smack just long enough for me to challenge him to a race, right here, right now, in the parking lot at Hardee's. Mitchell flinched but only because Sergeant Phillips was there. Bad time to get shown up but an even worse time to talk shit and back down. After polishing off my burger and fries, we made our way to the parking lot to throw down in full gear.

We lined up, with most of EXPO and the Sarge watching, and, after a rumbling belch, off we went. It was over quick and there were no surprises, for me anyway. I was clear across the finish line as Mitchell was just getting out of the starting block. As the years have passed the margin of victory becomes greater. I smoked him and he never heard the end of it.

Let it be said that there were few dull moments at EXPO. However, we had few funny ones on the job. This was my favorite:

We were tasked with helping to conduct a search warrant. If an officer does not attend the briefing before executing the warrant, the officer is totally in the dark as to the situation. We were to serve this warrant on a barbershop located on the eastside that was as raucous and colorful as any clip joint Ice T ever managed in a movie and all the detectives were in on this one. Unfortunately for EXPO, a bunch of us had court or more pressing business that kept them away from the briefing and had no idea whatsoever that the barbershop was under surveillance or that shit was going down that had nothing to do with shaving.

When the remainder of our crew assembled and was ready to roll, we converged on the barbershop and executed a textbook tactical entry. The occupants were rounded up and marched out the front door in the walk of shame so that the search could be conducted. Lo and behold, the first person to be escorted from the premises was one of our own, Officer Baker, who was holding a plate of barbecue and with a look on his face of sheer shock and awe.

As he made his exit surrounded by officers, Baker shouts, food flying from his mouth, *What's goin' on, y'all?*

Shout out to Officer Tim Lewis:

We were rolling in the EXPOdition-- Lewis, Brown, Frazier, Sawyer and I-- and we were looking for trouble in all the right places. We were in the badlands of Hazzard County, where we came upon a vehicle that was clearly trying to steer clear of us. We tailed them as they made fast turns and accelerated to put some distance between us. Turning onto Otto, we picked up the vehicle which had just zig-zagged into Henry Lane, where the driver bailed and lit out on foot.

The Expedition was still moving when I jettisoned from my seat and hit the ground running. I am moving in for the kill when suddenly I came to an immediate halt. As I came through a fence my radio cord got caught up in chain link and jerked me backwards like in the cartoons. I

110

snapped off the cord and took off running again and that's when I heard a gigantic thud followed by a high-pitched scream and then dead silence.

I cornered the house and saw the subject I had been chasing laying face down in the grass with Rufus Brown cuffing him behind his back. Sawyer was standing over him and calling for EMS, and Lew was spinning in circles, waving his hand and yelling, *Start me EMS! 10-18!* (Code for Big Hurry).

I got Lew to stand still long enough to see that he had dislocated his finger while taking down the subject. That had to be painful for the both of them. Tim Lewis was a big guy and as tough as they come but this was not his highlight reel moment. Sawyer had keyed the radio as Lew was yelling in pain and the high pitch-- which just did not match his quiet and menacing presence-- was broadcast countywide. Half the department showed up on the scene thinking we had a officer down and the other half thought we had rescued a damsel in distress.

The good part of this story is we found out why the subject did not want to speak to us: he was holding enough marijuana to turn on half of Hazzard County. Good pop for Lew. Bingo!

It is no secret that money talks and there are few places that I am aware of where it speaks louder than Savannah, Georgia, where justice is whatever you can afford. There is also that dirty rotten double standard that dictates that misdemeanant sons and daughters of well-heeled connected people get a free pass for the same offenses that send poor kids to jail. Here's an interesting story involving the son of a SCMPD Captain:

The Savannah College of Art & Design holds a concert in Forsyth Park every year, the purpose of which is to celebrate graduation, but the rest of the city crashes the party that takes over the center of town. Naturally an event of this size requires heightened police presence even though the school employs its own security force. EXPO was called in to help supervise the concert of 2006.

K-Fraiz and I were checking parking lots for concert-goers doing anything of substance, no pun intended. We had pulled onto Jefferson Street, which runs parallel to the park, when out of the corner of my eye I spy a young man emerge from behind a dumpster with a bottle in his hand-- a minor open container violation-- but justifiable cause to look a little closer. We pulled up just as the subject returned to a red SUV where a pile of his friends gathered around. They were all very young, like under-21 young, so we carded everybody and the next thing we know we're turning up more alcohol and a bag of marijuana. But before K-Fraiz and I can get this sorted out, one of the subjects leans in to inform me that one of his parents is a captain with SCMPD.

Now I have a fucking headache.

Making matters worse, we turn up an eyeglass case containing a pill wrapped in cellophane, which takes the stop from a little bit of weed and underage drinking to felony possession of a controlled substance; double fucking headache. Before charging the suspects and cuffing them I called Capers and let him know that I had a captain's kid on the hook that by all rights should be going to jail like any other kid. And regardless of what anyone will tell the reader, a situation like this always creates a certain amount of-- how can I put this judiciously-- "political uncomfortableness".

112

Personally, I could give a shit what anyone thought or said about how we were going to handle this situation. Even before Capers showed up at the scene K-Fraiz and I had already decided our course of action: These kids were going to jail on the misdemeanor marijuana and alcohol charges and the pill was going to be logged for further investigation, which is code for No Follow-Up. Hanging a felony on a college kid could have life-altering effects and this was a clear-cut case of stupid college kid, not street-wise drug dealer. The fact that one of them had a mama with bars did not influence our decision one bit, but Mrs. Grogan and Mrs. Frazier did not raise any dummies. Doing favors for Captains never hurts an officer. Even if we really did not do any big favors here-- such as cutting all of them loose-- it would appear we had.

Sergeant Capers showed up at the scene and we advised him of our decision. Capers did not bat an eye. It's your call, he said, and he agreed with it.

The Downtown Precinct Commander who was doubling as Incident Commander for the concert-- and who was dear friends with the mother of our suspect-- arrived minutes later. She arrives and starts giving us a political stump speech about how this was our call and no one was going to try to influence our decision or influence our decision on how to exercise discretion or what to charge or what not to charge. Again, the decision was already made so there was no real need to go any further with it.

I told the Commander that we were booking the Captain's kid and his cronies with misdemeanor possession and underage partying and losing the pill in the paperwork. I could tell by the look on her face that

113

she agreed with the decision and by the ever so slight nod of her head in the affirmative.

The Captain whose child was at the center of all the fuss did not show up on the scene even though they were on call and in the vicinity. Neither Frazier nor I ever spoke to them about the incident. And to be perfectly honest, I would handle the same situation the same way today and for the same reasons as in '06.

The ironic karma of this episode took years to come around: Sergeant Capers, after being cited Supervisor of the Year in 2006 for his leadership role with EXPO, ran into some issues with Chief Berkow and ended up being demoted and reassigned to the Intelligence Center as a Firearms Investigator. And it just so happened that the captain whose son we had spared was the commander of this unit.

Hold on, I know what the reader is thinking. I'm not finished:

The U.S. Marshal's Office launched an operation in which Capers played a supporting role and during said operation ran up on a kid who was in possession of a small amount of marijuana. When I say small amount, it was barely enough for a stingy joint. The kid was scared shitless and was not the target of the operation so Capers rubs out the weed and tells the kid to go home and be good to his mother. And for reasons none of us will ever understand, the Captain called Capers on the carpet and reprimanded him for dereliction of duty.

Here he had shown the very same discretion we had shown the captain's son for a much greater offense and the beneficiary of said favor was leading the charge to hang Sarge. When the veterans of EXPO heard

114

this deplorable tale it became abundantly clear to us all that SCMPD is a place where politics changes in an instant and that the concept of loyalty is dead. Further, it was a clear indication of far worse conditions to arise in the near future.

* * * * *

It was June of 2006 and unbeknown to us, EXPO was headed for extinction. I will get to that in a minute. But I am reminded of the day when Sergeant Capers took the podium at roll call, briefed us on our daily mission and then said we needed to take a vote. Chief Lovett had announced that an award was being given out and that someone from this unit would be getting it. Sarge said he was not going to make the call, rather he was going to let us vote as a unit. The only stipulation, he added, was that the unit had to decide between two officers: Brown and Grogan.

In the heartbeats between Sarge saying that he was going to let us vote as a Unit and that we had to decide between two officers, I, along with everybody else, automatically thought he was talking about Rufus Brown and Josh Hunt. When he said my name I almost fell off my chair. I felt the blood rush to my face and my throat tighten as if I were being choked. I did not know what to say or do but before I could do it, Brown spoke up:

Ain't no vote, he said, pointing straight at me. *It belongs to that man right there. I got all the medals I need.*

And that was it. No questions asked. No further discussion. Rufus had spoken and I received the 2006 Southside Optimist Club SCMPD Officer of the Year Award along with Nathaniel "Nate the Great" Kirkland

115

III, my brother from another mother on B-Watch. We received a nice plaque and were treated to a luncheon held at the Fairmont. I was truly humbled to receive the honor because I'm supposed to say that, but to have it come while being a member of EXPO made all the difference; that Nate was co-recipient made me feel like I was doing the right thing because he was the most thorough cop I ever worked with and admire him to this day.

To be perfectly honest, I think now as I did then that any award handed out in 2006 should rightfully have gone to Rufus Brown. As they say in Hollywood around Oscar time, to have been considered for the award is honor enough. The real compliment to me was being mentioned in Rufus Brown's category. I have received awards from the Military and police but the fact that Sergeant Capers, a man I have the utmost respect for, considered me to be in the same class as Rufus Brown and for Rufus Brown to defer the honor to me are the two greatest compliments I have ever received.

I know I come off as an arrogant bastard sometimes but I will take this opportunity to say it once and for all: I will always consider myself to be a capable police officer and better than average but I am simply not in the same league as Rufus Brown. I have seen the best that law enforcement has to offer, from small town Sheriffs to Federal Bureaus of This and That, and Brown is the best that ever picked up a gun and a badge. And should the reader deem that I have not provided enough reasons to think so, please, be patient. I am not finished telling you about my hero Rufus Brown.

*   *   *   *   *

It was September 2006 and SCMPD was gearing up for robbery season, otherwise known as the holidays. Chief Lovett moved assets around the chessboard that is the map of Savannah's historic district in forming the Robbery Intervention Detail (RID) using members of SWAT, EXPO, the Intelligence/ Gang Unit and the K-9 Unit in cooperation with the Sheriff's Department. Lieutenant Lee from Downtown Precinct was placed in command of RID, a good choice, having had years of tactical experience, and just a damn fine cop.

The first weekend that RID was in business we were tasked with maintaining high visibility downtown adorned in our bright Yellow Shirts and riding around in marked patrol cars; it does not get more highly visible than that. Lieutenant Lee ordered us not to jump corners. He wanted us to concentrate on the entertainment district, to be seen by anyone who might be thinking of doing something stupid, and he did not want us tied up on petty arrests when Part 1 calls went out. So we hit the hotspots in our louder than life Yellow Shirts along with our pals from SWAT in their Mr. Green Jeans suits, and we were seen in great numbers riding the streets and lanes. RID was a conservative Protect and Serve strategy that is employed by many cities but it was not the EXPO way.

I remember being seated next to Rufus Brown during our initial briefing and flinched when he raised his hand, which was unusual for this man of few words, given his complete understanding of the chain of Command and respect for it. Before he uttered the first syllable I could tell what he was thinking if only because it was a theme we had discussed before and practiced successfully for the prior nine months:

117

I understand the high visibility thing, Brown said, *but I suggest that while it is still early in the evening that we hit the neighborhoods to deter any activity on tap for tonight.*

Lieutenant Lee tuned out Brown like he was on a different frequency. *No jumping corners,* Lee repeated. *Remain highly visible downtown and be ready to respond to radio calls.*

I raised my hand, following Brown's lead, and suggested the same thing, only in a slightly different way: *The only way to prevent robbery is the same way we stop a domestic; either we have to know it is coming or be right there when it happens.*

I got the same response from Lee that Brown got. And then Lee cut us loose. It's important to note that LT. Lee didn't dismiss Brown and I because he didn't understand and maybe even agree with us. LT. Lee was real police and it was obvious to me that he had been given the same directive we had been given. I know it didn't come from the Chief but remember there are majors and captains between the LT and the boss.

I do not remember why, but I was in a car by myself. Friday turned into Saturday and activity on the street was winding down. We were out in full force at 0230 for club closing at 0300. I was in the thick of it all on Broughton and Jefferson, and cruised around the corner to check on pedestrians making their inebriated way to the parking lot.

I'm riding the lane when what should appear but a totally naked man running around like he has lost his ever-loving mind. I will never forget the look on his face. This wasn't some jackass who drank too much and went streaking on a bet. It was clear by his expression that something

118

cataclysmic was unfolding. When he ran straight for me I knew it wasn't some sort of college prank.

Perhaps the reader is unaware, but it is not unusual for victims of street robberies to be forced to disrobe, robbing them not only of their money and jewelry but of dignity as well. I looked where the victim was pointing and spotted the brake lights of a Grand Marquis whose driver was looking over his shoulder with eyes as wide as only they can get during adrenaline induced moments. I knew it was a go and I knew what to do: I got on the radio and advised all Units to respond and then set off in pursuit of the suspect.

The suspect backed out of his parking space, threw the car in drive, spun the tires and blazed a trail through a crowded State Street to Montgomery, then turned north toward Broughton. I caught up to him when he slowed down to make a turn but as he raced down West Broughton I saw sparks fly as he sideswiped several parked cars. Officer John Nevin was coming east in his unmistakable Dodge Intrepid and Captain Caveman had that look of absolute disgust that this fool was disturbing the peace. My anxiety was heightened when the pursuit made its way onto MLK, where pedestrian traffic was heavy. The suspect took a wide sweeping left turn onto Bay, accelerating into the turn and causing the car to spin. I came to a complete stop and watched the car complete a 360-degree spin out and then again and again.

The Grand Marquis came to a complete stop and I jumped out of my unit thinking the suspect was going to jump out and run. I got a good look at the driver, expecting to see an older dude and was surprised to discover he was baby-faced. I'm yelling at him to stop but there was no

119

quit in this kid. He righted himself, looked towards Bay, and floored it, tires smoking, and off we went again.

I was trying to close in as he hit the top of the ramp to the viaduct and lifted off, sparks flying from the rear bumper as the car took flight. I lost sight of him when he crested the hill but I saw the crash at the bottom of the other side: there was a bright flash, sparks, and fire followed by a loud explosion and a huge cloud of dust. I had seen too much of this kind of thing to think for a second that the chase was over. Vehicle disabled, sure, but that did not mean that the suspect who had stuck a gun in a man's face, forced him to strip down in a parking lot, taken his clothes and money, then led us on a high-speed chase through downtown was not going to miraculously jump out of what was left of a stolen car unscathed and run away into the night.

I pulled up to the scene of the crash, swerving to avoid power lines falling into the street. I realized then that there was not going to be any foot chase: the car was nearly folded in half, the driver immobile, lying between front and back seats, with power lines draped over the car.

I looked up to find Sergeant Rowse standing there with his arms folded and the same unexcited look on his face that I typically encountered. I knew I was going to have to explain all this in my report. Adrenaline was still coursing through my veins and I began to rattle off my justification for the pursuit when Rowse cut me off.

Nah, boy, you're good, Rowse said. *Unless there is no gun in there, then yer fucked.*

A big smile creased his face and Rowse grabbed me by the shoulder. *Good work, kid*, he said.

We found the suspect's weapon and the victim's clothes on the floorboard of the wreckage. The car had been halved when a transformer was dislodged after impact with the utility pole and crashed down onto it. The driver was identified as Fledell Edwards aka Tank, and the car he had been driving was stolen. Tank was wanted in Garden City for charges stemming from a separate carjacking incident, possession of drugs, false identity, and fighting with police. Of all the incidents that RID were involved in during its brief existence, the Edwards case was the most notorious.

I teamed with McBride on the fifth anniversary of September 11, and rode around in an attempt to be highly visible when we spied a guy riding a bike without lights at the south end of Forsyth Park, so we stopped to have a chat with him. He was making every effort to remain cool and calm but I noticed he was slightly shaking. I got out of my unit and the closer I came to the subject the more he shook. I put my hand on his hip and discovered the reason for his unsteadiness: a 9mm Hi-Point that I relieved him of. McBride ran the subject's criminal history that showed prior robberies.

We will never know how many robberies RID's high visibility prevented but I know how many suspects we apprehended and it was the result of proactive policing. The man we arrested on this occasion did a stint in federal prison for this offense. Parenthetically, he was one of two murder victims in Kayton Homes a few years later in a case worked by my former partner Josh Hunt.

RID came to an end shortly thereafter and EXPO returned to our normal operation. We were still in that highly competitive mode where stats did not matter and the quality of the arrest was everything: severity of charges and amount of evidence confiscated. We met up before moving from one neighborhood to the next and discussed how we were going to approach and engage for maximum effect. We could not wait to fish the honey holes and some of us shifted prematurely, sacrificing safety in numbers, in order to get a chance at the first bite.

We were back in West Savannah in the Clearview neighborhood, preparing to shift across West Bay to the Augusta Avenue corridor. Clearview was not easy to police because, like the projects, once we were there word spread so fast that by the time we entered the neighborhood everyone who was out went in. We stopped anything and everything on suspicion but it was dead calm on this particular evening-- and then the call went out.

The Woof Wagon sounded like they had their hands full. Neither Young nor Mitchell were cowards and they never blew up the radio to make out a situation to be more serious than it was. There was a certain urgency in their traffic and I could feel that they needed help. All EXPO Units flew around Clearview but there was no sight of them. It was then broadcast that they were already on Augusta Avenue, ahead of shift.

I bounced across Bay at an obscene rate of speed and found Young and Mitchell with their bright Yellow Shirts covered with the unmistakable orange stain of OC Pepper Spray standing in the middle of Augusta and Dunn, where they looked like they had just run a marathon and their sinuses draining from their faces to the asphalt. It was truly a sight to behold. There was a busted bike lying in the middle of the street but no suspect.

Where'd he go?

Slow everybody down, Mitchell said. *We're good.*

Other Units were arriving and taking in the scene. *We're good, we're good,* Mitchell kept repeating.

Hell no, we weren't good: there was obviously someone in the area who was most certainly suffering from the same OC effects presently plaguing Mitchell and Young. So we set out in search of the culprit until we found a young man simmering in pepper sauce and snotting all over himself in the bushes near a school. He was taken into custody for obstruction. EMS arrived to flush his eyes and lessen the sting of that godawful stuff. When the suspect was stabilized I placed him in the cage of my unit.

I could feel his white hot stare in my rear view mirror. *You slapped me and sprayed me for no reason,* the suspect said to me.

I had nothing to do with it, I said.

Muthafucka, you slapped me and sprayed me for no reason, he repeated.

Look, I protested, *I am not the cop who slapped you or sprayed you. I am the cop who had EMS clean you up and who is going to drive you safely to jail. Maybe you still got pepper spray in your eyes and can't see clearly. But trust me, I didn't slap or spray you.*

The suspect continued: *You slapped me, you sprayed me and you killed my cousin.*

Wait. What? Who was your cousin?

Tank, he said.

Long pause.

Man, I didn't slap you or spray you, I said.

The defense rests.

*   *   *   *   *

One of the hallmarks of Operation EXPO was a warm and fuzzy feature that I called Forced Friendship Days. Sarge realized that the best way to deal with alpha males acting like teenaged girls was to split up teams and make us ride with other officers. Sometimes he did it in order to curb bickering and at other times to bolster production by having top producers teach underachievers new tricks.

I recall one particular Forced Friendship Day when Capers decreed that Officer Young and I should become besties. I had always gotten on with Young, a good guy, a funny guy, with no issues. But I really didn't know him all that well and this was my first time getting to see him up close and personal, and for him to see how I got down.

124

Young did the driving and we started our shift in West Chatham, and it started immediately. *Man, I don't know why we even out here,* he complained. *There's nothing going on out here at eight o'clock in the morning.*

That kind of rationale always bugged hell out of me. Crime can occur anywhere, anytime. I had learned while training under Robie Walp that if a cop is willing to look for trouble in Savannah, It is always somewhere to be found. I took Young's attitude for laziness and lack of commitment to the EXPO cause, for which I had no patience. We were supposed to be an elite squad of hard hitting, crime fighting machines and I learned this day from my new friend that not all of us saw it that way.

I tried to explain to Officer Young that It, meaning Crime, is always out there and that it's up to us to find It. But Young remained unconvinced. At our first meetup I told Sarge that I needed a new friend for the rest of the shift, bailed on Young, and rode with K-Fraiz.

I did not have to explain the EXPO philosophy to Frazier. He had been on a few months longer than me and we had a similar approach to Policing the street. The only differences between us was that K-Fraiz was six-foot-ninety, 300 pounds, and I'm five-nothing and a Big Mac shy of 95 liters. And because he did not have to worry about size issues, K-Fraiz was as aggressive as anyone on the force and the force was always with him.

So we rolled through our sector of the Wild West and picked up on an old dude hot-footing it along Bay at a rapid pace, the kind where he is trying to move faster than his worn out wheels will permit. The old dude turned out to be our pal Mister Bell. What surprised me was that I had

125

never seen him away from his post at The Alamo. Neither had Frazier, who had the same inquisitive look on his face I had.

Fraiz, I said, *you ever seen Mister Bell away from The Alamo?*

Nah, said Fraiz, *and he's gettin' it too, ain't he?*

Mind, Mister Bell wasn't doing anything illegal. He was just doing something unusual for him. We could not come up with a reasonable articulable suspicion for a legal stop. So we continued to drive past Mister Bell even though every nerve in my being told me he was up to something.

I just gotta know, I said to Fraiz.

So I stopped the car and got out. *Mister Bell, I said, can I holler at ya for a minute?*

Mister Bell stopped dead in his tracks. He looked left, right, then straight at me.

You good, Mister Bell?

Who, me?

Yeah, I said. *You got a second?*

Note: That was another Tamargo-ism I adopted. It's how we kept everything non-custodial. A citizen doesn't have to speak to a cop. If they are not breaking the law they can flip me off and keep on going or ignore me completely. But I tried to talk to subjects as if it were social, not

126

business, and tried to avoid using commands like "Stop, police" unless absolutely necessary.

Man, I've never seen you outside of The Alamo before, I said. *You good?*

Who, me? Yeah.

You sure?

Yeah, yeah.

Then I noticed Mister Bell kept feeling around his right pocket. This is what is known to police as telegraphing, where subjects who are armed or in possession of contraband will unconsciously touch that which concerns them.

Mister Bell, you making me nervous, I said. *Got any weapons on you, sir?*

Why? No.

I reached out and patted him down around the waistline where most weapons are commonly concealed. Finding nothing, I moved to the pants pockets and found a large lump. I couldn't tell what the hell it was but by the way his body stiffened I knew it was something he wished he didn't have on him at that particular moment.

I might have some dope on me, he said.

127

Can I remove it from your pocket, I asked, which I did only to be polite, and found a bag of crack that felt like more than an ounce and another bag with a few lines worth of powder.

I radioed 1110 and Sergeant Capers responded.

Bingo, Millen and Bay, I said.

Brown and Sawyer dropped by to see what the winnings were.

If you see Young, I said to Sawyer, *let him know It is always out here.*

* * * * *

It is a little known fact that EXPO avoided the public housing projects. It was rare that Sergeant Capers allowed us to venture there and some of his reasons did not have to be explained. I was trained in the projects, where I could articulate anything that was going down and come up with a reason to stop just about everyone. And maybe that was one of Sarge's reasons for making the projects off-limits, to keep them from becoming concentration camps. What most critics often overlook is that the projects are full of good people who are on the struggle; the trouble comes from parasites who feed off the young women and the elderly who are supposed to be there. The Savannah Housing Authority is diligent in their efforts to keep trouble out of the projects but it is hard to rid the vulnerable of parasites that move in and set up house in exchange for ready cash.

128

EXPO got the green light to ride Hitch Village and Fred Wessels one night. Floyd called out that he was approaching a group of guys gathered at the picnic tables by the basketball court. The park was closed and there was no lawful reason to assemble there. It was something that the Housing Authority frowned on but did not stringently enforce. As Floyd approached, the boys took off running and Floyd called out their direction. When I heard Floyd say north, I had a good idea where they were headed: the north side of Fred Wessels, at East Broad and President.

Rounding the corner from Oglethorpe onto East Broad I heard the unmistakable sound of gunfire and saw a flash that lit up the buildings facing Burney Drive. Talley sped up and just as we hit the middle of the block on President, I saw a male subject run out from between the buildings, see me, throw something on the ground, turn and run. I chased him all the way across Oglethorpe and behind the buildings on Avery, where it was poorly lit. I saw him duck behind a staircase where he was trapped and gave up.

After a quick pat I walked him back to the unit and secured him, then went to where I saw him drop the object and found a .38 caliber revolver. I looked into the chamber and saw a garden variety of ammunition-- some of the rounds were regular brass .38 Special, some were .357 with a grey casing-- with none of the rounds expended. Obviously, this wasn't the gun that fired the shot and probably not the guy who shot at Floyd.

Nonetheless, the kid was only 17 and had no business with a gun. I searched him and found a mixed bag of bullets in his pocket matching the assortment in the pistol. This is as open and shut a case as it gets. Yet, almost three years later, I found myself at the trial in Chatham County State Court over this case.

129

Cases like these typically get pled early on but this one went to trial because his mother came up with enough money to contest the charges. I testified to these facts and the jury found the defendant guilty. I crossed the courtroom to the other side, extended my hand and sincerely wished the defendant luck. He would not shake my hand and his mother turned her back to me.

I hate that this kid did not own up to his mistakes, a minor misdemeanor that could have gotten him and others hurt. This kid was not a hardened criminal, just a gangsta wannabe, a mama's boy with no respect for The Game. It sticks with me to this day.

Compared to other accounts in these pages the reader might be thinking that this one is not among the best anecdotes. Oh, but I am not done. The aftermath of this case was what made it memorable:

The entire EXPO Unit was ordered to headquarters and herded into the squad room right after the shooting incident in Fred Wessels. Sergeant Capers greeted us. He grabbed my arm and steered me away from the group with a look on his face I will never forget: biting his lower lip like he wanted to fight.

Who shot? Which one of you motherfuckers?

Whoa, Sarge, I said. *We weren't the ones doing the shooting, they were.*

Let me smell your gun, he said.

Now I've been in combat and have responded to many shootings, and witnessed many crime scenes in the course of my career, but never have I had anyone ask to smell my gun because they did not believe me when I said I hadn't fired it. I was taken aback and didn't know what to say. But a complaint had been filed with the department that officers barged into the projects and shot up the place for no reason, no reason at all. Even though I did not see who fired the shot I know it wasn't one of us because we discussed the event in the debriefing. Sergeant Capers went to the trouble of counting our ammo and found that we were all good.

It was apparent that someone had filed the complaint to keep cops out of the projects, not because we had shot up the place without provocation, but because they did not want us there. Maybe it was some punk or some victim who was put up to it, but it only made Policing the projects that much more politically treacherous and a more dangerous place to live in the process.

As of this writing, I am not active duty law enforcement. But not a day goes by that I don't stop whatever I'm doing and flashback on what I was doing eleven years ago. The mind winds down like an old clock and some of the memories run together. But one of my favorite recollections isn't so much about the size of the bust or the names involved but because we were altogether in one place doing the job we loved and were so very good at:

We loaded up the Meat Wagon-- me, Lew, Jack, K-Fraiz, Baker, Sawyer and Randy Smith, with Brown at the wheel-- and we rolled into Tatumville primed and ready for action. We came upon a group of guys standing out in front of a house and as they made us, a runner cut from the herd and disappeared into the back yard. Brown dropped the load and each

131

of us grabbed one of the lads before they knew what hit 'em while the rest of us followed the leader. It was quite a sight: an entire van of 200+ pound men had emptied out, neutralized the area, and some took off at full speed chasing a kid with a decent head start. It was a sight that had become all too familiar at this point.

I remember seeing the bright yellow lettering on the back of the black shirts in front of me and thinking this would make a hell of a photograph. We flew over a fence and towards a tree line, the canopy of which cast dark shadows over the terrain.

I heard a voice holler, *That's right! Run away from the light! That's what we want you to do!*

Seconds later, Baker had the runner in custody.

He dropped a paper bag along the way, Baker said. So we retraced our path while Bake searched the suspect and found an ounce of crack in his pocket. We found a paper bag filled with what felt like a pound of marijuana. Bingo. We took photos holding the trophies with the meat wagon as a backdrop. But the impression formed in my memory is much more vivid. The mind's eye opened like a camera lens and I remember the episode frame by frame.

It was a successful take down and no one was injured. Mission accomplished.

Cloverdale and Carver Village Heights were EXPO stomping grounds but later in my career they would become important places to me if only because I worked with an ATF Agent named Toby Taylor who became one of my closest friends. Toby was the consummate undercover Agent, a shape-shifter who had an uncanny ability to make even the sharpest players in the 'hood believe he was just some big dumb country boy with an odd fascination for rap music; he was anything but. He played the part so well that he could say anything, even openly insult black dudes who took no offense because they believed him to be simple-minded.

While working an undercover sting and posing as a mascot that hung around a head shop because he supposedly had no place else to go, Toby once said something so offensive to a black man that his lady said to Toby, I'm gonna pray for you.

But Toby taught me how to cross-reference different cases and connect the dots. After all, Savannah is a small city, and as the joke goes, "We all cousins in Slow-vannah."

I was part of the unit that worked Operation Ruffian, which targeted a street gang in Carver Village calling themselves the Carver Village Thoroughbreds (CVT), hence the title of the op, a clever play on the word Ruffian, which was also the name of a legendary racehorse. This case endeared me to the neighborhood, especially Hadley Street, which ran parallel to the better known Gwinnett. Only part of Hadley is inhabited and there is an unlit cut-through where people avoid being noticed. Toby and I formed our daily plan of action while cooping near a lone single-story cinder block house where we were watched by a four-legged sentry that, like Mister Bell, could always be found seated at his lookout in front of his building. This was his turf and he made us keenly aware of it.

He was a rat terrier, maybe with a touch of Jack Russell in his family tree, and had a range of human-like expressions. He did not bark

133

and he did not bite but we could see it in his face that we were not welcome. Then one day while Toby and I were sitting and thinking, we watched as a man on a bicycle rode through the cut and attempted to pass Gangsta Dawg too closely. The little rat bastard jumped up and tore into the cyclist's foot and he pedaled away like his life depended on it. The dog went back to his stoop and laid down with a look of perturbed self satisfaction.

Gangsta, I said, nodding at the dog. And from that day on we called him Gangsta Dawg or GD, for short. Gangsta Dawg just chilled in the cut; that's what he was about. We saw him in the same spot every time we dropped by and his demeanor remained unchanged. Mind, we would say hello to Gangsta Dawg but he wouldn't be bothered by us as long as we kept a respectful distance.

Game respects Game.

Then one morning it came to a head: We were getting an early start in Carver Village and I stopped at Burger King to grab a croissan'wich, sausage and egg, no cheese. Two for four dollars. I sharked the first one and done. Toby brought a sack from home and wasn't interested. I put the spare croissan'wich in the glove box for later.

We pulled into Hadley, and spotted Gangsta Dawg laid up like he'd been out drinking the night before and was dead to this world. He looked like he could use a good meal. I tried to bridge the gap with GD by unwrapping the croissan'wich, crossed no-man's land, and tossed it to the ground in GD's direction, close enough where he could grab it but not so close that he might think I was throwing it at him.

134

Gangsta Dawg reared up from his slumber, gazed at the croissan'wich, and then looked at me. He looked at the food again and then looked back at me a second time. He did not lick his lips. He gave me a scowl that said: *Fuck you, police. I ain't no snitch.*

Then he slowly got to his feet and walked away, leaving the food untouched.

Pure gangsta.

*   *   *   *   *

In the fall of 2006 there was a significant event where an officer was assaulted and his weapon taken by a bad boy named Juwuan Lee. Chief Lovett formed the Bad Boys Task Force in an effort to locate young Juwuan and return the weapon to its rightful owner. Since EXPO flexed the Departmental muscle, the Chief staffed his task force with Sergeant Armando Tamargo, Detective Robert Gavin, and APO George Gundich, the first two being experienced in Homicide and the third a first-class head-splitter. Well hell, all three were head-splitters but this Gundich was more than just a brute. He also knew how to make solid cases and he knew how to run an effective operation that reached a successful conclusion.

The Bad Boys got a tip from an informant that Juwuan Lee was standing out front of the car wash at East Broad and 37th Street. He was supposed to be wearing a green shirt. The Bad Boys saddled up and took a dirty unit to be washed and put an end to this whole mess.

I remember the call going out from Sergeant Tamargo that their target was fleeing from the location in a stolen black Volvo station wagon.

135

Everyone on the radio knew who Tamargo was talking about-- the guy who had knocked out one of our own and taken his weapon-- and who was now evading capture in a stolen car. Every unit on the move wanted a piece of Mr. Lee and it just so happened that the muscle of the Patrol Division was on the street.

Traffic continued to update minute by minute as units flew ahead and tried to cut off any pass where Lee might be headed. We knew which way he was headed but still had no idea where he was going; he drove as if he didn't know, either. The pursuit moved from Central Precinct to Downtown, across Anderson, and northbound on Montgomery, where traffic backed up and helped us gain ground on him.

The dodgy thing about car chases is this: If an officer is not in policy while pursuing, you're fired; if the officer is in policy and has an accident, you're in trouble; if the officer is in policy and a citizen has an accident, you're in trouble. Bad guys on the run do not play by the rules but police do not have that luxury. It is a constant decision-making process: Does the risk to the public outweigh the danger?

This is what cripples modern-day Policing, especially in Savannah. More often than not, SCMPD let the bad guys go because it was not worth the risk to the public. Life is not a TV show but too many people think police should act like cops on TV that have everything wrapped up nicely at the end of 30 minutes or an hour without the stars getting so hurt that they can't come back in the next episode. It doesn't really work that way in the real world and Savannah gets pretty real.

I got to MLK and Bolton when I heard that the target was bottlenecked on Montgomery. Rufus Brown was first to reach the car. He

136

opened the door and grabbed the driver just as the car ahead moved enough for the Volvo to slide by. The driver floored it, the B post separating the front door from the rear door slammed into Brown's side, pushing him sideways as the car lurched forward.

Brown held on to the driver for a full block while being dragged down the street until his injuries forced him to let go.

To this day I have never been able to figure out how Rufus got up, got into his car, and was the first one behind the target vehicle in pursuit. He hasn't been able to explain it to me, either.

The pursuit continued west and headed down Gwinnett, a major artery with a number of escape routes: access to MLK, I-16 West, 516, plus a hundred little turn offs in Carver Heights. There was so much traffic on the radio updating speed and direction that I can't remember who said what. That is until Brown asked the magic question: *1113 to any Supervisor, is Deadly Force authorized?*

The radio went silent waiting on the response.

Negative, Sergeant Phillips replied.

The pursuit continued down Gwinnett and turned south on Stiles Avenue. Policy dictates that there be no "daisy chain" and that only two Units can actively pursue the suspect vehicle. I was fourth in line and there were 20 behind me. Fuck policy, this guy hit a cop and took his gun, and had just now dragged one of our EXPO brothers with a car. This pursuit wasn't ending until this guy was caught.

137

Down Stiles to Ogeechee, then to Liberty Parkway, the vehicle made a brash move. Rather than slowing to take the upcoming left-hand turn onto the parkway, he decided to cut through a dirt parking lot in front of a roadside produce stand. The uneven ground broken up by rocks and the roots from huge oak trees were his undoing, causing the vehicle to bottom out and blow the front tires.

The driver jumped out before the car came to a halt. The target, a dark-skinned black male in a green shirt ran across Liberty Parkway into the parking lot of a grocery store. He grabbed a woman as she was loading her bags into her car, but was swarmed by Yellow Shirts and Blue Uniforms. Rufus got his hands on him first. I joined in to subdue the suspect. I remember it looking a lot like a Bugs Bunny fight: a cloud of dust, a hand here and a foot there, with a Yellow Shirt and then a Blue one, and a few painful cries. And then 10-95: Suspect in Custody.

After cuffing his hands behind his back I rolled over the suspect and quickly realized this is not Juwuan Lee. What was more important to me was where I looked next: Leaning against a wall was Superman holding his side with a pained look on his face I had never seen before.

Brown, I said, *you okay, big dude?*

Nah, was all he said, and then slowly slid down the wall.

Sergeant Ernst ran inside the Dollar Store and grabbed anything and everything he thought might come in handy in making Rufus more comfortable, including a blanket. He had tried to pay for the items but the clerk insisted that he take them for free.

138

Rufus had broken ribs.

He took the rest of the day off.

He was back on the job the following day.

Man, I said, *why don't you just chill and rest a while and heal up?*

'Cause if I lay down too long, I might not get back up, Rufus replied.

Inspiring, that's all I can say.

Two other officers were seriously injured in an accident during the pursuit. Kenny Brewer and Shermonica Beatty wrecked at Stiles and Gwinnett, and went through the windshield. The accident essentially ended Brewer's career and sidelined Beatty with a broken pelvis, tragic reminders that pursuits are not fun and games and sometimes police are seriously injured doing a dangerous job.

Juwuan Lee was still on the loose but we got the second man on the local Most Wanted list: Cornell Morgan, who was wanted for assault during a home invasion. Tamargo and Gavin continued to make Lee a top priority and eventually tracked him all the way to North Carolina, where they pursued him and took him into custody.

One of the biggest concerns for the department was that the service weapon that Juwuan Lee had stolen was still out there somewhere and might be used in the commission of a violent crime; not good publicity for SCMPD. The recovery of the weapon was a top priority and Job One on Sergeant Capers' punch list. Capers had grown up in Savannah, knew Lee's family and some of his hangouts, and went to Lee's uncle, a known player, for assistance.

Capturing Juwuan was important to the department, Capers told the uncle, but recovering the weapon is important to Savannah. We want our weapon back. If it does not materialize, and right soon, I'm going to let my dawgs loose in your neighborhood until the weapon is found, he said.

Capers hadn't been gone from uncle's house fifteen minutes when he received a telephone call from an anonymous source telling him to look for a brown paper bag out front of Central Precinct. Mission accomplished, weapon recovered, and EXPO stayed on the other side of town that night; a gentlemen's agreement.

Our reputation for getting after It and getting the job done was so widespread and effective that neighborhoods invited us to drop by and hang out on street corners just to keep the peace. Old people flagged us down and told us that our presence in their neighborhood made it possible for them to once again sit on their front porch and enjoy the evening without fear of being shot or molested or witness to a crime. We could be seen coming from a mile away, the Yellow Shirts, like we were walking, talking yield signs.

* * * * *

It all came to an inglorious end in November 2006. The Lovett interim ended with the hiring of Michael Berkow as the new Chief of police of SCMPD and with it, EXPO was disbanded. It was widely reported that because of shortages on Patrol that the officers of EXPO should go back where they came from and ride beats, and it then became apparent that the new chief did not see things eye to eye with the assistant chief.

I cannot speak for anyone else but I took the disbanding of EXPO as a giant "fuck you" from Berkow to Lovett, and that the new chief was sending a clear message that SCMPD was his department now. What the general public was unaware of is that a few months earlier, when it was announced that Berkow would be hired and before leaving his position as Deputy Chief in Los Angeles, he sent out an email blast to every single member of SCMPD and asked us to send him our resumes and take this one-time opportunity to let him know what we liked and disliked about the department.

Berkow received several responses from officers about EXPO, criticizing the manner in which it had been created, who was selected, the brutality of our methods, and that we generated bad cases. And all of it combined was nothing more than an elaborate, orchestrated smokescreen for the fact that command was pissed that they had no say in what EXPO did. Purely on the strength of these complaints, and before being in place long enough to get his seat warm, Berkow put the blast on EXPO and pulled the plug.

"New Chief Disbands SCMPD's Muscle Unit," was the headline in the local paper, and reading it was like reading an obituary of sorts. I don't think I read the whole article but I remember the headline. There was no fanfare or farewell for having achieved our goal in reducing violent crime in Savannah. The majority of EXPO was sent to Central Precinct's Crime Suppression Unit and the rest became the foundation for a new CSU in Southside Precinct. Sergeant Capers unceremoniously returned to West Chatham Precinct. I was the only member of the Unit who returned to my old Precinct and rode a beat which wasn't an issue, especially since I went back to B Watch.

Over EXPO's 11-month existence we made 1,466 arrests, seized 35 pounds of marijuana and 20 ounces of cocaine, confiscated $34,000 in drug money, and took 93 guns off the streets of Savannah. In addition to all that, EXPO had been instrumental and played a critical role in gathering intelligence in major cases, including the Jennifer Ross Murder.

EXPO was credited, begrudgingly, as being the main variable that led to a 15.2% reduction in Part 1 crime throughout Chatham County.

And here's the odd thing: Over the next several years, attempts were made to replicate EXPO's success but Units like the Neighborhood Task Force (NTF) never had quite the same effect as EXPO nor did they earn the same reputation.

Through these same years I have frequently found myself arguing the merits of EXPO with cops and Robbers and the man on the street. I explain to cops that EXPO's success cannot be replicated because of its unique chemistry and how a department that relates to itself entirely on race once had a unit where race was not a factor.

Rufus Brown didn't care if I was white and I hardly noticed that Floyd Sawyer was black. Josh Hunt never thought once about Tim Lewis being black and Sergeant Capers-- other than for logistical reasons imposed upon him—couldn't have cared less what color any member of his Unit was. At no time while on EXPO did I ever feel any racial tension. Not even our harshest critic will stoop so low as to accuse us of it.

With the sole exception of the soldiers that I fought alongside in Baghdad, at no time in my life have I felt closer to a group of men than I did as a member of EXPO.

Ask me why EXPO cannot be replicated by today's SCMPD and I will point out that the department does not have the type of leadership that will step outside the box of orthodox thinking and make it happen. Independent thinkers among the captains and lieutenants are a vanishing breed but they still answer to the top. The greatest hope, as I see it, for the department as it moves toward 2018 lies with Majors Kerry Thomas, Devonn Adams and Rob Gavin. These guys are police, not mere administrators. Their qualifications go far beyond any training they have had and the system has not yet crushed their drive, although they run a danger of it happening.

SCMPD is in good hands with Captains Ashley Brown, John Best, Lenny Gunther and Lieutenants George Gundich, Mike Izzo, Greg Ernst and Alex Tobar. Together these seven officers have all the tools to take Metro where it needs to go if only command would empower them to do it.

There is a staff shortage, as of this writing. But there is enough tale nt to form a strong core. I cannot say if the rank and file still have the drive to take the amount of pushback good cops receive for doing what they do best.

I have complete faith in all of them.

Chapter Six
One Hitter Quitter

On EXPO's last official day in existence, I was on my way to pick up a plaque we had all chipped in to get for Sergeant Capers when he called me:

You got a college degree?

I do, I said.

Well, he said, *you're going to homicide.*

A couple minutes later, I got a follow-up call from Captain Merriman.

You still interested in coming upstairs?

I am, I said.

How soon can you be in my office?

Ten minutes ago, I replied.

Let's make it noon, he said.

I arrived at 11:30 a.m. We talked about what I knew and, more importantly, what I didn't know. Nevertheless, the captain said he needed someone to start work right away. The meeting concluded with his promise to call me the next day. I never heard another word from him. Turns out that the spot I was going to fill never opened up because the detective I was to replace blocked the move.

Soon after, I was in the process of finishing a class to become a Police Training Officer (PTO) when Sergeant Tamargo informed me that I was being temporarily assigned to CNT. Apparently, the information I had supplied turned out to be almost identical to what CNT received from the ATF, and Chief Berkow thought I might have something to offer in Operation Raging Waters.

Toby Taylor was the case Agent for the ATF on Operation Raging Waters. We were friends from the moment we met and with the sole exception of Sergeant Capers, Toby has had the single greatest effect on my career in law enforcement. A gifted tactician, he has a unique ability to analyze complex situations and come up with simple solutions to correct them. I have never, ever worked with any law enforcement officer with a better understanding of the big picture than Toby Taylor.

For the first few weeks we met at CNT headquarters and briefed strategies. After the meeting I was paired with the CNT Agent who logged evidence or made phone calls that had nothing to do with Raging Waters. I attempted to relieve the boredom by riding around in plain clothes in my marked unit to try and scare up a little business. I had a modicum of success at collecting and verifying information that we already possessed. The highlight event came when we apprehended one of the Fergusons on the lam for kidnapping his own child from daycare, a custody dispute from Hell.

No sooner that I fell into a coma-like routine at CNT, they pulled the plug-- as they were wont to do-- and decided they'd rather work a wire tap with DEA than go swimming in Raging Waters.

Classic CNT.

I reported to Sergeant Rusty Smith and said: *I know you don't need me on the wire, so what should I be doing?*

I got nothin' for ya, Smith said. And then he turned his back and walked away for emphasis.

I don't think I have ever been more disgusted by a lack of leadership in my life. But it did not stop there with Smith. I went over his head to Lieutenant Greg Mitchell:

I know you don't need me on the wire, so what should I do?

Keep doing what you're doing, he said, LT Mitchell has always been a positive and upbeat guy,

What I had been doing wasn't very much: I continued to show up for the morning briefs and that's when Sergeant Oglesby told me to come to work for him. Sergeant O was with TRAP, the SCMPD Vice Unit, and he hooked me up with my very own unmarked unit and turned me loose on the streets I loved so much.

Sergeant O taught me more about finding, developing and signing on informants, and conducting controlled and undercover drug buys than hundreds of hours of training and a couple years of experience ever could.

146

I may have been a slow study but Sergeant O was a big believer that a team gets more done than any individual. He never expected credit for his work but he took tremendous pride in the work of his officers that he trained and developed; that list is long and distinguished.

TRAP targeted subjects connected to the Fergusons and dope houses in hot spots that the ATF had identified. We had a tough time getting close to these targets until Teeone "Spyro" Spencer was killed. Spencer was believed to be one of the shooters in the James "Murdock" Ferguson homicide.

My former partner Josh Hunt, who came over from violent crimes to help with Raging Waters, developed enough intelligence to support a search warrant on a locale where Deaubry "Dub" Gardner was holed up. "Dub" was the top dawg in the Waters Avenue Crew. He was the odds-on favorite suspect in the Spencer homicide, having been identified as a main target of Operation Raging Waters. When the warrant was executed, Gardner and two associate gang members were found in possession of several firearms, including two that were linked to Spencer's murder.

The success of this warrant and the arrests of the members of HVP and other gangsters delivered the message that the task force was finally getting some serious results. After 27 arrests combined with all of the good work from Sergeant Oglesby's TRAP Unit, Chief Berkow pulled the plug on Operation Raging Waters.

A meeting to wrap up the Operation was held between the Sheriff of Chatham County, the Director of CNT, Chief Berkow and his Command Staff, representatives from the U.S. Attorney and District Attorney's offices, Special Agents in Charge from division level federal

147

agencies, including the FBI, Secret Service, DEA, and my old buddy Bobby McCormick, ATF's Resident Agent in Charge of the Savannah Field Office. At this meeting I was to present the arrest statistics and the nature of these arrests. Josh Hunt was to wrap up the meeting with an explanation of how search warrants lead to the arrest of murder suspects.

I stood before the single largest assembly of the highest ranking Law Enforcement personnel in this part of the world and made what I thought was an impactful speech. I didn't sweat it too much, really. I've never had a problem speaking before higher ranks, especially having worked directly under a 4-star General with whom I had established a warm, personal relationship. I must admit, however, that I found the presentation infinitely easier to deliver by focusing on my pal Bobby Mac, who was just an all-around great guy.

My presentation was illustrated by the PowerPoint of everything we accomplished throughout the entire Operation, at the insistence of Sergeant Oglesby, who always gave me a chance to shine at every opportunity. He had seen my presentation and only added one slide. It read:

TEAM: Together Everyone Achieves More

It was the code SGT Oglesby lived by and drilled into every officer he trained. I think now as I did then that the Policing profession needs more Sergeants like Lavon Oglesby.

When I was done with my presentation and stepped aside for J-Hunt to conclude, Chief Berkow then took the stage to congratulate the entire Raging Waters team.

148

Mission accomplished, Berkow pronounced, and the crowd went wild.

CNT will continue to follow up on the leads but this wraps up Metro's involvement in Operation Raging Waters, he added, and the crowd continued to applaud.

It was a great operation all around, Berkow smiled. *It's great for everyone, except Grogan, 'cause he's going back to the street!*

The audience laughed not because it was funny but because the chief had delivered my fate like it was a punchline. What was funny to everybody else in the room came as a shock to me. I had no idea, at this point, that I was going back to a beat. I had done a ton of work on this operation and my reward was to be embarrassed in front of everybody.

I remember staring at the crowd and locking eyes with Homicide Sergeant Mike Izzo, who looked like he was watching a train wreck in slow motion. Apparently, I wasn't the only one in the room who failed to see the humor. Worse, it was the biggest slap in the face of my professional career.

I was sent back home to the Downtown Precinct where B-Watch had changed but not as much as I had. Sergeant Robbins and Sergeant VonLoenfeld were the new shot-callers and I went back to my old ways. The personnel had changed some but guys like Santana Willis, Sean Horton, Nevin and Arango, Eric Blazer and "Uncle Mike" Embry were still around. It was also about this time that I got to work with my twin, Rico Anderson. Rico had just come back to the street from CNT and we compared notes, they were the same. Don't get me wrong: I was still

149

working Hitch Village and I was still highly aggressive. I continued getting to know all the players and their game. But I had learned how to put cases together and no longer pounced on the first indiscretion that I saw.

It was Robbins who taught me more about how to work arrests into larger cases. He also instilled the idea in me that the Watch was more important than any single officer. He and SGT O were both old school and its men like them that keep traditions alive. SGT VonLoenfeld took up the lessons at that point to teach me the finer points in articulating a stop. He also gave me a new ability to explain my ways and means of operation. After a few months of what I thought was solid progress, I was tremendously disappointed to learn that I had been passed over by three other officers who had been moved upstairs to detective, including one of my EXPO brothers.

So I simply went back to doing what I do: hit the streets. I went back to my old beat and did what I had always done. I found that in the absence of direction and when things aren't going my way in police work, hitting the streets was the best way to stay focused.

I pulled into Hitch Village and spotted a young man who was on the Public Housing Ban List. He was already in full stride before I could even roll down my window to speak with him. He ran and I ran after him. He ran faster, but I knew my beat and where he was going. He ran upstairs to a second-floor apartment where his baby's mother lived and went inside. I ran to the side of the building where I could see both front and rear entrances. He did not come out the back so I waited until backup arrived. Then I knocked on the door of the apartment.

A young woman answered the door and I told her I wanted to speak to the young man who had just entered. After a few minutes of the usual he's not here, I have no idea what you're talking about, I asked her if I could come in and have a look around. *Sure*, she said, and stepped aside.

The apartment layouts in Hitch Village were all the same: living room to the right; a hallway leading to 2 or 3 bedrooms; a bathroom; and past the living room was a kitchen with an exit. I went through each room, looked in all the usual hiding places: closets, cupboards, under beds-- but I couldn't find this guy anywhere. I looked for a crawl space in the ceiling, vents in the bathroom, but found nothing large enough for a grown man to fit through. My back up came up with nothing; it boggled my mind.

Baffled and frustrated I stood still and listened, hoping he would do something to give away his hiding spot. Nothing. Just as we were about to give up something caught my eye: I looked down at the air vent for the central air conditioning where the two tabs that held the vent in place were pulled out. Kevin McKoon saw it at the same time and when he pointed at the vent. I opened the vent and McKoon shined his flashlight. Two hands popped out and a voice said, Okay, okay, don't shoot me. 10-95.

As we drove to jail the suspect told me that he knew what I was after and that he could help me.

You don't have any idea who and what I'm after, I checked him.

Then he started rattling off the names of everyone on the target list for Operation Raging Waters who hadn't been caught yet.

151

Before we arrived at the CCDC we had entered into a business arrangement. He became a trusted informant and in the process he earned my respect. With his help, ATF was able to disassemble a criminal organization that was distributing cocaine by the kilo throughout public housing in Savannah.

I continued to work the streets as I always had and developed other informants. I went back to working midnights and remember a particular occasion when I received a call from one of my informants asking me if I wanted to buy a Cadillac. I could tell he was trying to be cool and so I assumed whomever he was with had stolen the car. I asked him how much and he relayed that the guy wanted $300. So now I know my informant was with someone in a stolen Caddy. What I didn't know was that this car had just been stolen out of the parking lot of one of the most prestigious inns in the historic district and hadn't been reported stolen yet.

I told the informant to meet me at East Duffy and East Broad, where there is a small park that was notorious for drug dealing and other nefarious activities. I called Shermonica Beatty, who was riding Beat 2, for backup.

I had to come up with a reason to stop the car and hoped a situation where they could not flee would present itself. Luckily, that situation arose when I saw a white Cadillac driving down Duffy with no headlights on, passing right in front of me as I was stopped at a sign. The driver pulled behind a parked car, blocking a quick getaway. I pulled up alongside as I called it in on the radio. The vehicle was now contained.

I jumped out and approached. My informant was in the passenger seat so I played it like this was just a routine traffic stop. The driver was

152

in a state of shock, his eyes as round as softballs. I tried explaining to him that the only reason I stopped him was because of no headlights. As I talked to him, Beatty approached the passenger side. Then I noticed the driver's hand was inching toward the shifter.

I told the driver to turn the car off and he went straight for the shifter. I told him a second time to turn off the car but he continued to make his move. I reached across him and grabbed his hand just as it made contact with the gear shift as Beatty pulled the passenger out of the car.

The driver pulled the shifter down and my mind raced: here I was, leaning into the passenger compartment of a stolen vehicle, face to face with the suspect, my feet barely touching the ground, my right hand reaching across the steering wheel on his hand, and he is about to put this thing into reverse and accelerate with me hanging out the window.

I had visions of Rufus Brown with his broken ribs and of Josh Hunt, who had been in a vastly similar situation with Stanley Hall, and it was then that I realized that I had over-committed but there was no turning back now.

I planted both feet on the asphalt, released my grip with my right hand, and twisted with every ounce of thrust my 210-pound body could muster, and connected with a left hook that Smokin' Joe Frazier would have been proud of, what the gang back at EXPO dubbed a "One Hitter Quitter".

The vehicle never made it into reverse and the suspect was taken into custody. He admitted that he had stolen the car and that his passenger had nothing to do with it. It was another hour before the rightful owner reported the car stolen so that we could return it.

I received a string of accolades from the auto theft detectives and my sergeants for this arrest and felt that I had re-established myself on B-Watch. I always went to work everyday with the feeling that I was there to contribute but I had that What Have You Done Lately mentality. I was always trying to make that next good arrest or the next big case.

Like everything else, however, this too, would come to an end. And the incident that convinced me that it was time to leave SCMPD occurred shortly after a group of juveniles broke into the Kayton Homes gym:

Bunch of kids vandalized some computers and made a general mess of the place, just kid shit. Property crime detectives worked the case and asked Warren Pippen and I to help them track down the suspects. Pippen was a hell of a cop and the Public Housing Officer in Kayton at the time, and between the two of us we knew all the kids in this vicinity.

The Detectives gave us a name and an address off of Bee Road, where we found the suspect in question, a young man all of 16 but already 200 pounds and 6-foot tall. A big kid, but he had a kid's eyes and in street terms looked softer than marshmallow shit. With him was his mother, who quickly became defensive and irate that she did not want her child speaking to police.

I tried to explain that detectives were working a case and her son's name came up. I tried to explain that if he didn't have anything to do with it that the quickest and easiest way out was to cooperate with detectives and clear his name. It took fifteen minutes of heated discussion before mama calmed down enough to agree to letting me take her son Downtown.

154

Property crimes detectives and a Downtown Precinct sergeant showed up to supervise as I was walking the kid to my car.

As I reached for the door handle to the backseat, the boy-- who was not under arrest and not in handcuffs-- asked me if he had to ride in the cage. It was a good question. After all, he was coming in voluntarily and a juvenile, at that. Seemed like a perfectly reasonable request, to me. But what made my decision for me was the look in his eyes: he was scared. I sensed that this was a defining moment in both our lives.

Go ahead, man, I said. *Sit up front.*

A property crimes detective ran over to me with an urgent message: *Supervisor says the kid has to ride in back.*

Hey, man, I said to the kid, *not your fault, but my boss says you gotta ride in the back.*

The kid complied and I went out of my way to hold a light-hearted conversation with him on the way downtown. I had a bad feeling when I introduced him to a detective who dismissed me, saying, We aren't going to need you anymore.

I went downstairs and ran into SGT Coates, my shift Sergeant.

So you want to tell me what happened?

Just finished a transport for the Detectives and they don't need me anymore so I'm 10-8, I reported.

I was told something about an illegal transport, he pressed.

155

There was nothing illegal about it, I said, slowly getting pissed. And then I explained all the reasons why there was no harm and no foul in letting a 16-year-old kid who was not under arrest ride in my front seat.

Fill out a Form 48, the Sergeant said, *then get back to work.*

I filled out a report of the incident and heard nothing about it for a few days. I was still pissed but it looked like nothing was going to come of it so why fuss? Five days later I'm walking into the Precinct for one reason or the other and the Sergeant who had the issue with the transport called me over. Now here's a supervisor that rarely spoke to me yet seemed genuinely pleased to be addressing me.

Remember the transport the other day? I wrote you a counseling about it so you need to sign off on it, the sergeant said. *No big deal.*

I looked at the statement citing a violation of the Prisoner Transport Policy as well as a general order.

The kid wasn't a prisoner, I said. *Neither was there a violation of any general order.*

No big deal? I had only one negative counseling statement in my entire file, with reference to missing a court date, and that was highly debatable. I didn't want negative statements filed against me in general and certainly not for a good call like this in particular.

With all due respect, I'm not signing that, I said to the Sergeant.

156

We'll see about that, the Sergeant said and grabbed me by the arm like I was being taken me into custody.

The Sergeant walked me back to the Lieutenant's office and had me tell the story of The Illegal Transport. The Lieutenant looked at me as if he too, was having a hard time coming to terms with the nature of the offense. And when I was done with my recitation, he thanked me and gave me leave. I could see through the blinds of his office window that the lieutenant was clearly on my side as he pointed to the document and held out his hands palms up as if to say: the officer has a point.

I knew that's what he said when the Sergeant grabbed the paper off his desk and stormed out of his office and out the front door of the Precinct without saying another word to me. The Lieutenant leaned out and told me to hit the streets.

I was on my way home and had made it as far as Price Street when my Precinct Commander, Captain Long called me on the radio: One Eleven to Two Bravo Four, Two Bravo Four, Signal 17, which meant Bring Your Happy Ass Back to the Precinct.

I returned to the precinct to find Captain Long had joined the party.

I'm very disappointed in you, Captain Long said to me. *You used very poor judgment and we take officer safety very seriously.*

He was a big kid and your gun was within easy reach, the Sergeant chimed in.

157

I am making every effort to keep my responses short and respectful but this was testing my limits. *Ma'am*, I said, *that counseling has nothing about officer safety in it. It's about a transport. And as soon as the Sergeant said the kid needed to ride in back, I put him in the back seat.*

He was a big kid and your gun was on the side where the kid was sitting, the Sergeant said again.

It's a question of judgment, Captain Long said, but did not complete her thought before the Lieutenant came to my defense.

The counseling statement makes no mention of officer safety, he said. It hasn't even been mentioned, up until now.

The Lieutenant's speed bump did not slow down the Sergeant's argument. Sarge continued to caution me about the proper manner in transporting suspects and how this kid could have overpowered me.

My head was spinning. While I couldn't figure out where this was coming from, it really didn't matter. I'm standing there listening to my decision-making skills being shredded over something miniscule in comparison to some of the really dumb shit I had done, and that's when I pointed out the obvious-- obvious to me, anyway:

I routinely jump out on multiple suspects in Hitch Village, I began, and I've arrested suspects with warrants when I should've waited for backup. I jumped through windows of stolen cars as they pulled off and got pats on my back. But now I am accused of exercising poor judgment when it comes to officer safety because I was going to let a kid, a child,

158

who wasn't under arrest, ride in the front seat of my Patrol car because he was scared?

I did not give the captain or lieutenant or sergeant the opportunity to answer before I concluded my argument: *If I can't handle a sixteen-year-old kid, I don't need to be wearing a badge*, I said, and reached for it as if to remove it from my chest.

But before I could remove it, Captain Long quickly reversed course.

That's not what I'm saying, she said. *I am simply pointing out that you need to make better decisions.*

For a moment I could hear my mother, former teachers, and any number of girlfriends echo that response. We parted with Captain Long advising us all that she would look into the matter further.

I never heard another word about it again.

But the climate of the department had changed and I felt it shift on that day. I was passed up for detective, I had been called a liar by Holmes and Sergeant Hughes, and CNT said I refused to turn over informants. I could read the writing on the wall, so I left.

Chapter Seven
Yes! We Have No Gangs

Denial is the worst enemy of police.

So said Detective Jose Ramirez in an article published by the *Savannah Morning News* in 2005, with reference to the presence of gangs in Savannah, and the Department's inability to come to grips with their existence. And with that interview, Jose's days with the Department were numbered.

Detective Ramirez worked as the sole Gang Investigator and was perhaps the first to identify gangs such as the Hellhole Dwellers (HHD) and the Tatumville Terrors (TVT). He gathered a mountain of intelligence at a time when no one in Savannah, including the police Department, wanted to acknowledge there were gangs here. His biggest mistake occurred when he dared to answer Chief Flynn's questions about gangs when his supervisor, Sergeant Katrina Hughes, could not. I would make a similar mistake later in my career.

I would later get to talk to Jose about Gangs when he was the Vice President of the Georgia Gang Investigator's Association (GGIA). GGIA had become a powerful force in the prosecution of gangs in Georgia and work with the state legislature to create a powerful law that called for serious penalties for violation of the Georgia Criminal Street Gang and Anti-Terrorist Act.

I had no knowledge of gangs other than what I had seen on TV and heard about back home when the streets of Hartford erupted in a war between Los Solidos and the Latin Kings. It wouldn't take long before I was overwhelmed by the gang presence in Savannah. While working the projects, graffiti told the story of, if nothing else, the existence of gangs. In Hitch Village I saw, in addition to graffiti everywhere, tattoos and t-shirts emblazoned with HVP and HVC: Hitch Village Posse and Hitch Village Committee. At the same time I saw more guns and drugs than I had seen in the first thirty years of my life.

As a point of clarification, both Fred Wessels housing project and Hitch Village sit to the east of East Broad Street, the eastern border of Savannah's Historic District. The end of Oglethorpe Avenue separates Wessels in the middle and is surrounded on both sides of the street. Oglethorpe ends at Randolph Street, which tees and serves as the only street to separate Hitch from Wessels. By continuing onto Hitch Drive, you enter the heart of the Village. Fred Wessels and the west side of Randolph is referred to as "up top" and Hitch Village and anything east of Randolph is "down bottom". And should you become lost or confused, all you have to do is check the bottoms of the buildings for the gang signs advising you whose turf you are trespassing upon.

Camouflage was Hitch Village's favorite son. He had been born in Savannah in 1981 and at the ripe old age of 18 recorded his first rap record with a group called Crime Affiliates. After selling more than 50,000 copies, he was in line for a major recording contract when he was busted for crack cocaine and the deal died on the vine. At the top of his game Camouflage opened for the biggest acts in the biz, including Ludacris and Trick Daddy and Ice-T. He was gunned down while walking his son outside Pure Pain Recording Studio on West 37th and Florence at the riper age of 21, and thereafter his likeness could be found all over Hitch Village on t-shirts worn by residents of all ages.

161

While working with EXPO, I saw similar gang graffiti in other neighborhoods. On the westside, I saw "LVK" (Low Valley Kings) in Cloverdale, and "VBS" (Villa Boy Soldiers) in Carver Village. In Cuyler-Brownsville, "CBV" or "41st Family" was everywhere. The "Craw Boyz" of Yamacraw Village and "TVT" (Tatumville Terrors) were prevalent. On the eastside near Waters Avenue, I saw GSP (Gwinnett Street Posse) and the red five-pointed stars of Piru or Bloods. I didn't pay a lot of attention to these markers because EXPO wasn't looking for gangs; we addressed whatever popped up. We did not stop to identify gangs or gang members, even though the Intelligence/Gang Unit would ride with us a few times and photograph individuals that we stopped, interviewed and sometimes arrested.

It wasn't until EXPO came to an end that I began to get a better look at gangs in Savannah. ATF had identified three major gangs that were causing quite a stir across the city. They were shooting up the town and killing off their competition and all of it was gang related. Operation Raging Waters centered around Hitch Village, Waters Avenue and Gwinnett Street, and their respective gangs. This war was all about drugs and territory. While I was called to provide intelligence about a few of the drug dealers that I knew in Hitch Village, I figured out who was who and what positions they held in their gangs, especially in HVP. I identified the shot callers and watched them to find out who was second in their chain of command. During Operation Raging Waters, I spent most of my time chasing individual gang members and laying the groundwork for assembling intel on their organizations.

When I joined MAC E, I learned how to put a gang case together. I was assigned part-time to a major investigation that the ATF was conducting in Statesboro with the police Department, and at the same time

162

I was learning all I could about a gang that operated in Liberty and Long counties, calling themselves "DPG" or the Dog Pound Gangstas. I identified individual gangstas and as I came into direct contact with them during arrests or search warrants I noticed the same graffiti and gang paraphernalia that I had seen in Savannah, including the TIP/RIP t-shirts and tattoos. But now I was inside gang members' homes where I saw photographs of gangstas wearing colors and flashing signs and how it all fit together. While investigating DPG, I acquired my first gang bible, complete with gang rules, hierarchy, associations and memos of drug deals. At this point I had enough to put together our own Operation.

ATF Special Agents Toby Taylor and Lou Valoze were busy running Operation Statesboro Blues and preparing to start up a new Operation in Brunswick, so Al Cato suggested that we take our findings directly to the FBI. After all, gangs were supposed to be their expertise. We discovered that really wasn't the case but the FBI and DEA came through with some buy money which eased my budgetary constraints and then paved the way to run repeat offenders through Federal Court instead of Superior Court.

I learned a valuable lesson here: Even though I could prove these guys were a gang and operated as a criminal organization, as far as prosecution went, it was more beneficial to proceed against them as individuals based on their criminal histories than it was to prosecute under RICO statutes. As with Operation Raging Waters, we prosecuted gangs under the Organized Crime Drug Enforcement Task Force, which meant the U.S. Attorney's Office prosecuted them for lower level offenses that did not ordinarily meet prosecutorial guidelines. We were also able to draw from a larger pool of funding that allowed smaller agencies like MACE to go after larger targets and not break the bank.

I could go on at length about OCDETF and how the Feds have more money than the locals, but suffice to say, it was a huge advantage to have that kind of support and for more than just financial reasons. Federal sentencing guidelines mean serious time for repeat offenders and there is no parole; felons don't just walk back out. Operation Invisible Fence was a huge success and in the end, the U.S. Attorney's Office for the Southern District of Georgia reported to the national OCDETF board that the Dog Pound Gangstas were dismantled by this Operation and impounded. And according to my sources, that had never been done before in Georgia.

Upon my return to SCMPD, I was assigned to West Chatham Precinct, which covers a wide area of country mixed with small developments on the outskirts of Savannah. I spent the majority of my time in Carver Village, which was covered by "CVT" and "VBS" painted on the streets, on trees, and just about every other building. There were also roll calls painted on pavement: a list of fallen gang members, including the name of a young man who had been shot by police. I also noticed an army of young men wearing t-shirts with photos of incarcerated friends and emblazoned with "CVT" and Free So and So written underneath or RIP/TIP shirts that said something similar.

As I began putting together intel on CVT, I got a call from my old friend Toby Taylor, asking me if I had anything going on. I told him all about Carver Village and that I thought it made for a perfect investigation; Toby agreed. A few days later I got a similar inquiry from my old friend Sergeant Capers-- excuse me, Corporal Detective Capers-- advising me that he was interested in getting his own Operation going.

That's right: After having been named Supervisor of the Year by Chief Lovett for his masterful direction of EXPO, Chief Berkow deemed

164

Greg Capers unfit to be a supervisor and busted him in rank, then reassigned him to the Southside precinct. Capers would later go to the Savannah Area Regional Intelligence Center (SARIC) where he was a Firearms Investigator. Capers wanted nothing more than to get back in The Game. I filled Capers in on what Toby and I had just started and invited him to join the party.

Together we identified an organization heavily involved in armed robberies, auto theft and narcotics distribution. Not the easiest offenses to investigate, often complicated, and did not always lead to a suspect's home base. And when it comes to narcotics, investigations can be as grand as manpower or funding will permit. But in the opinion of Sergeant Oglesby, an investigator is limited only by their imagination so I did the only thing I knew how to do and did it well: hit the streets.

I had the help of an informant in making small controlled narcotics purchases and drafted a handful of search warrants, the service of which further developed intelligence that connected gang members and linked gangs to other gangs. During one such warrant we came across a gang bible belonging to G-Shine, a spin-off of the Gangsta Killa Bloods (GKB) gang, one of the most violent organizations in America.

When I moved upstairs to homicide, there was a rash of murders in Hudson Hill that appeared to be connected to the Gangsta Disciples, a national gang rooted in West Savannah. With the murder of Rebecca Foley during a botched robbery on the southside, we established that the shooters were members of the Bloods and shortly thereafter, found evidence of outlaw motorcycle gangs.

165

Savannah does not like to admit that gangs reside within her city limits; bad for tourism. And in a town where more than 12 million tourists visit each year, leaving behind more than $2 billion, Savannah will go out of its way to avoid investigating gangs so as not to scare off the tourists. In a police department of 600, there have only been two or three detectives assigned to the Gang Unit at any point in time. Even so, the Unit rarely spends 40 hours per week investigating gangs. Homicide attempts to fill the gaps by investigating gangs independent of the Gang Unit, but intelligence does not flow between them. Worse, the chain of information is broken between the patrolman on the beat and investigators.

Theoretically, this information could be shared on the SARIC website or even by email between officers, but in my 10 years of experience with SCMPD, I never saw it happen once. Not once.

Intelligence is how crime is solved. Intel cannot be gathered and stored for any length of time; it is fluid and must be constantly updated before its expiration date, which means the department must be pro-active and in constant search of information.

The single best illustration I can point to is the Outlaws, one of the FBI's Big Four Outlaw Motorcycle Gangs, along with Hell's Angels, the Mongols, and the Pagans. The FBI asserts that outlaw biker gangs support themselves primarily through dealing drugs, trafficking in stolen goods, and extortion, and are in a never ending war over territory that yields $1 billion in illegal income annually.

The average Savannahian has absolutely no idea that the Outlaws have a chapter headquarters in Garden City, bordering Savannah to the west. The clubhouse is directly across the street from the third largest port on the east coast of the United States. But as long as the bikers do not cause trouble within Savannah's jurisdiction, they are immune from investigation by SCMPD. I guess because we don't see guys in biker gang cuts shooting people or riding around in stolen cars, they don't contribute to Savannah crime statistics.

By that same twisted logic, if we don't see guys standing on corners wearing red or blue bandanas and flashing gang signs, with pistols in their waistbands, then gangs don't contribute to crime in Savannah, either. It is this line of thinking and the lack of effort and ability to gather workable, prosecutable intelligence that causes Savannah to be constantly plagued by crime.

During the 2015 mayoral campaign, gangs were a major issue in the debates. At the conclusion of the final debate, I spoke with Mayor Edna Jackson and offered to put on a seminar for her City Council and the County Commission to show them the irrepressibly real danger that gangs present to the City of Savannah, and show them exactly what SCMPD is up against. I never heard from Mayor Jackson, and as of the publication date of this book, I haven't heard from Mayor Eddie DeLoach or either of the two city councilmen I solicited with the same offer.

Denial is the worst enemy of police.

Chapter Eight
The Return

The first major change in my life happened when my father died in 2009. He had never been sick a day in his life and then one day he was gone; an aneurism while watching TV. He was kept around on life support while doctors at Tufts University tried to figure out the extent of his injury and for all of his remaining days my family stayed right there with him at the hospital. I took that opportunity to say everything left to be said to my Dad.

How do you thank a man who had done everything for you?

I had a harder time saying good-bye. I could swear at one point while I was sitting next to him and holding his hand that I felt him squeeze me, but it is unlikely that he felt anything. I had been to war and seen death on a tremendous scale, but seeing my father on his deathbed was the first time I considered my own mortality. He died on October 7, 2009, and it had a profound impact on me.

I returned to MACE only to lose my boss and good friend Al Cato, who was unceremoniously removed from command. Cato was a gruff man, not really a touchy-feely kind of guy. The Chief Deputy of Liberty County and the Chief of the Hinesville Police Department decided Cato had served long enough and was burned out. At least, that was the explanation they gave me.

I'm sure, more realistically, Cato was axed because there had been confrontations with a couple of officers who did not appreciate his pointing out that their performance was substandard. Instead of supporting their commander, both chiefs opted to move someone else into the captain's position in order to help bolster their retirement. Regardless, Al Cato was one of the most dedicated lawmen I ever met and if they could remove him, I knew this was a place I did not want to be anymore. After all, Al Cato was the only person who agreed with me that gangs existed in Liberty County.

I read the headlines in April 2010 that Willie Lovett had been named Chief of the Savannah Metropolitan Police Department. I was thrilled for him and the department.

It was a shame the way Willie Lovett had been treated. After coming to Savannah's rescue as Interim Chief and crippling violent crime by more than 15 percent, his name was thrown back into a hat with five other candidates in search of a new Chief. A lot of phony reasons were proffered as to why Lovett failed to stack up after having performed above and beyond the highest expectations. To take the job away from him and give it to a white Assistant Chief out of Los Angeles was nothing more than the result of political pressure brought by scared whites with money who had bailed on Savannah but still ran it from remote bases in nearby townships.

Nevertheless, Willie Lovett satisfactorily completed police chief training in October 2006, just as his replacement was coming on board. Chief Berkow put Lovett in charge of criminal investigations, patrol, and special operations with a new title: Assistant Chief of Operations.

Odd, though, how the first thing the new Chief did was kill the single most effective operation in Savannah Police history and Lovett's signature accomplishment by gutting EXPO.

Berkow's stay in Savannah was short-lived: he failed to celebrate his third anniversary on the job.

I found it easier to be Assistant Chief of Los Angeles than Chief of Police in Savannah, Berkow said on his way out the door. *I understand the gangs and the drugs in L.A., but what goes on in Savannah just doesn't make sense*, he said.

It made sense to Willie Lovett. And in September 2009, Willie Lovett became Interim Chief for the second time in his career. His name was thrown back into a hat, this time with 90 other applicants from around the country, and the search committee interviewed from a list of 10. It took six months for the committee to reach its final decision in naming Willie Lovett the next chief of police.

There was no mention of the fact that Willie Lovett was Savannah's first black police chief at the press conference held to introduce him to the public. It did not play a role in his selection, Lovett said, nor will it govern his decisions as chief.

I am the Chief of Police, and that's for everyone, Lovett said.

Mayor Otis Johnson focused instead on the importance of promoting from within the department, adding that in almost four decades, a chief had not been hired from within SCMPD. When you are part of an organization, there should always be an opportunity to move to the top spot, Johnson said. And when it doesn't happen, it has a cooling effect on those who aspire to the top spot.

Today, we're saying to all of the people on command staff that you have the possibility to become Chief of the Metro Department, the mayor concluded, *and we are setting that example today by designating Willie Lovett as the next Chief.*

Chief Lovett's new tenure was to begin with a clearly outlined agenda that had been developed by the search committee. Among the top priorities: developing a strategic plan to reduce drugs, gangs and guns, to include aligning the Counter Narcotics Team's policies and practices with Metro Police. It also called for the creation of a Narcocide investigative protocol using CNT and police to jointly investigate drug-related homicides. Another high priority would be reducing crime by repeat offenders and to explore the use of an electronic monitoring system to track offenders.

In the process of attending to this agenda, all concerned hoped that Willie Lovett would bring together city and county managers who had been at odds over the management of CNT.

The press conference concluded with a plea to the public from City Manager Michael Brown, asking Savannah to show its support and provide input necessary for the new Chief to succeed. *When the Chief makes a difficult decision, the public needs to support him,* Brown said. *I will be with him. You need to be with him.*

Chief Lovett was given the final word.

In the very near future, our job is going to get just a little bit harder, he said. *I say that because we do police work every day. That's our life. But if you have specific goals and objectives you have to reach, sometimes people are going to be unhappy.*

Undoubtedly, thoughts of his first interim assignment flashed through his mind, of EXPO, and having reduced crime by more than 15 percent by way of an unpopular operation, and the embarrassing manner in which his replacement had dismantled all the good he had done.

It's important for everybody in the communities of Savannah and Chatham County to know that there are going to be decisions made that are not going to be accepted by all, the chief concluded. *But as Mr. Brown said, you are with me now, please be with me then.*

That's all I needed to hear. I had been with Willie Lovett before and loved it. And if he was ready to pick up where we left off, I was ready, too. I promptly applied to Metro and went home.

I had to go through two weeks of department training, the same course required of every recruit fresh out of the academy but abbreviated. I was happy to be back home and felt like I was headed in the right direction. I ran into a bunch of guys I had worked with before and it was good to see them. I ran into my old precinct commander, now a major, and she made sure I got a regular police ID instead of a recruit ID; no big favor, but she made me feel welcome.

I called Mike Wilkins, whom I had worked with on Operation Raging Waters and was now a captain and Downtown Precinct Commander, and told him I was hoping to return Downtown. I asked him

172

if he could get me in his precinct. Captain Wilkins was as excited as I was. Again, I felt welcomed. But at the end of my two weeks, I was assigned to West Chatham Precinct and I was confused.

I called my old friend, Greg Capers. He already knew of my assignment and explained why: Lieutenant Katrina Hughes was Downtown and Capers thought I should avoid her. It seemed logical to me, and I had no choice in the matter, so off to West Chatham I went.

I vividly remember my first day back at Metro. I entered the back door to the annex, where I used to go during EXPO, and it felt like coming home. As I made my way to roll call I bumped into Ronald Dollar, whom I had never worked with on the street but was a fellow member of the Departmental Honor Guard. Big hug and I could tell he was as happy to see me as I was to see him. Good feeling, ended quickly.

I walked into the roll call room and scanned a bunch of strange faces I did not know. There were some guys who were going to be on my new watch and some guys decked out in the new CSU uniform, new to me anyway: navy blue and khaki polo shirts which I never cared for. Guess I was partial to yellow. Back in the corner I spotted the familiar face of Jeff Oliver, an original EXPO member, whom I acknowledged with a smile and a point of the index finger. Oliver gave me a quick nod and then looked away. Guess he wasn't as happy to see me; noted.

My new shift was a good mix of old and new. I knew the older folks and had no clue as to the younger ones. My old buddies Gene Johnson, Daryl Cone, Tony Edwards , Sean Horton and Russ Champion, who had also left the department and come back, were on the same watch

173

so I knew I had a couple of sounding boards. Either way, I was going to do what I always do.

I liked this watch. One of the new guys, Kyle Godfrey, turned out to be a ball of fire and we had some fun in Carver Heights. He hadn't been EXPOsed to my style of policing, but he quickly picked up on it. Godfrey could have gone places in the department but because he did not have a lot of patience and felt the atmosphere for advancement did not favor him, he left SCMPD altogether. No department can afford to lose guys like Kyle Godfrey.

I had been back less than three months when I got the call from Capers about getting something started. It was during those three months that I picked up off-duty security gigs in bars, a great way to make more money when there was no overtime. One of the guys on my watch hooked me up with Rachel's 1190 in Georgetown, a neighborhood bar where everybody knows your name. The owners, Rachel and Darrin, were two of the best people I could hope to meet. They were hard workers and it showed in every facet of their operation. I worked for them most Friday and Saturday nights for nearly two years, from 11pm until closing at 3 a.m. I also had a few drinks in that place.

It was right about the time when I made the decision to go back to Metro that I realized my marriage was coming to an end. I see no need to go into detail about the how and why my marriage fell apart but, suffice to say, we grew apart philosophically on the subject of how a home was supposed to function. I am no angel and accept full responsibility for my part in the breakdown.

Many observers of the manner in which I work and carry myself tell me that I come off as arrogant. I can only respond to that one way: I am extremely confident in my abilities and truly have shamelessly little concern for how I am viewed personally. I do, however, care deeply about how I am viewed professionally.

I have noticed a strange coincidence that my best friends have an extremely similar approach to their jobs. I admire the people I call friends and I trust that they respect me. My closest friend in the world is Toby Taylor and that friendship is based on our similar passion for how police work should be done. We pride ourselves in going after the people who make it hazardous for children to leave their homes and walk to the corner. Toby and I have gone to great lengths to ensure that grandmothers do not hesitate to allow their grandchildren to walk to the store and back. We may not have always succeeded, but we have never stopped trying and never will.

* * * * *

No one can talk about the Savannah Chatham Metropolitan Police Department and not mention race. Just as the department was divided at the time of the merger, it could also be said that it was divided racially. It became all too convenient to try and blame that on men like Willie Lovett, but I offer a more realistic cause: Race has become an issue for people who have no focus on the true mission of the police department. Police officers who are mission-oriented have no time to worry about what race other officers are; they put their energy into succeeding in their assignment.

Race rears its ugly head when officers who are focused on politics and self-advancement have too much time on their hands; the true cancer of any police department. Career Police Officers who sit back and watch as cops go out and hit the streets. Career Police Officers who point out how the strong man stumbles or where the doer of deeds could have done them better. They sit back and wait for the opportunity to tear apart what doers are doing and then try to gain favor by pointing out the mistakes real police make. They make their names by discrediting the actions of others instead of daring to be judged by their own actions. It is easier to rip apart and critique what other officers do than it is to be pro-active, and if one can do so and hide behind the emotionally charged feelings created by racial tension, then they have succeeded.

I'd even go so far as to say it's easy to sit back in safety and pick apart what guys are doing where it is not so safe. I have no tolerance for cowardice. I have always found that mentality to be sickening, no matter what the race of the offender in this case. Anyone who cannot stand on their own or for their principles has no place in a police department. I don't blame Michael Berkow for this mentality because it was prevalent in the department while he was at the top of it. But it was only when he became chief that I became aware of it.

I was always lucky to be a tweener, meaning that I was a white man with plenty of black friends. It has been that way with me all my life, from childhood through my army years and my stints in law enforcement to the present day. I do not care about race. I gravitate towards people who are all about getting things done and I have shied away from those who want nothing but to be destructive. While it's not hard for me to recognize how Southerners feel about minorities, I will never understand it.

176

Not only am I disinterested in racial agendas, I have always been surrounded by mission-driven men, especially when I was on EXPO. It was later during my second hitch with the department that I saw the frustration of guys who were all about doing their jobs. I had always heard about officers being promoted purely because of race but I never paid it much attention. I saw guys who I thought were exceptional officers passed over and officers who I thought were terrible get promoted. I listened to the complaints and thought it was just sour grapes but I can nonetheless report there were many people who felt this way.

It wasn't until I saw officers who were clearly not up to the task of being Supervisors get promoted that I saw how significant the damage that was being done to morale. I can truly say, almost without exception, I was blessed to work for good Supervisors. It was when I worked homicide, though, that I saw the effect of poor supervision and what it did to aspiring hard-charging officers.

Detective is an assignment-- not a promotion-- at SCMPD. There is an interview and screening process but it really comes down to who Supervisors choose once they make "the list," which simply means the candidate is qualified. In 2012, there wasn't even a pay raise that came with an assignment to the Criminal Investigations Division.

I had felt the frustration of seeing other officers get picked for detective before me several times when I thought there was nobody more qualified than I was. When I finally made it to homicide, I saw just how unprepared other officers truly were: they had the title and position but they did not know how to work cases. In my opinion, they had not worked the street long enough to be prepared for what it takes to become a good Investigator. The same held true for supervisors. There were several sergeants who had real street experience but little to no investigative experience and would take charge of a scene then look to the detective to tell them what needed to be done.

Ideally, once an incident is reported, the first responding officer gets a quick assessment of what has happened and if it is serious enough the supervisor is called for a decision on how to respond. The emphasis here is on making a decision. If the supervisor decides to respond, they must determine whether detectives are needed: in the case of a shooting, death or serious injury, a violent crimes or homicide detective responds. But I can't tell you how many times I would get a call from an officer or a supervisor requesting detectives to respond to a 80-year-old with a history of heart trouble who was found dead in their bed. Nothing suspicious, just a natural death, but because the supervisor didn't want to make the decision they called in the detectives.

If there is nothing the supervisor can do, there is nothing a detective can do. And officers working under supervisors who have no idea what to do lose confidence in leadership, order becomes fragmented, and discipline erodes. Prime example:

I got a call from a newly promoted sergeant requesting that detectives respond to an aggravated assault where a gun was fired but no one was injured. I was in the middle of working a murder case with another detective but there was no one else on shift so I responded to the call. When I arrived on the scene the sergeant briefed me that the victims were in their home when a man kicked in the door, pointed a gun at them, and demanded money. The victims told the gunman that they had no money. So the suspect shot into the wall behind the victims and then fled.

The Violent Crimes/Robbery Unit at Metro is a completely separate unit from Violent Crimes/Homicide. Here I am, a homicide detective, explaining to the Sergeant-- who made $15,000 more per year than I did-- that this was a clear case of robbery or at least the criminal attempt at robbery. But in his opinion, what we had here was clearly not a robbery since money did not change hands. After explaining the law to him, the sergeant understood and agreed with me.

Anyone can make a mistake. But what got my goat was that this sergeant had been promoted out of the robbery unit. And it is this exact kind of thing that discourages subordinates when they see people who are not ready to supervise get promoted ahead of those who are ready, and this was by no means an isolated incident.

Just like any other profession, people with the right connections get promoted before more qualified candidates, but in police work, it affects the mission. When emotion and perception of race are mixed in, it kills morale. I was blessed to work closely with people who were focused on the mission and didn't have time to worry about race and politics. I also worked around a few people who should have been more focused on the mission and less on the other.

Chapter Nine
Sign of the Times

Looking back on my career in law enforcement in Savannah, I can't help but think about the irony of what it means to patrol the Downtown Precinct.

I spent most of my training period and nearly all of my patrol time driving down Liberty Street on my way to war in Hitch Village, strategizing the best way to enter the hot zone so that I could gain an advantage and get the drop on the bad guys before they could ride and hide. I did not realize until years later that I was passing by significant amounts of dope that was sitting in parked cars along the way with St. Vincent's Academy decals. Granted, the dope hidden in the glove boxes of these late model cars didn't contribute significantly to the violent crime in Savannah, but I can't help but wonder if I had spent the same amount of time and energy trying to search these cars if it might not have prevented a murder like Amber DeLoach. So many lives wasted. White lives, black lives, rich lives, poor lives-- all of them succumbing to the same undercurrent of erosion.

Savannah doesn't change much and when it does, change comes slow. In 2005 and 2006, the murder of a young black woman was mostly ignored, except by her immediate family, but the murder of a white girl with ties to a prominent businessman and a County Commissioner brought so much attention that the trial was broadcast on Court TV. In 2013, the murder of a young white volunteer fireman and the murder of a young white girl who was attending Savannah State University attracted the attention of a prominent car dealer six months later. He was so concerned about these two murders and the murder of a troubled young white man that he took out a billboard on East President Street, also known at the Islands Expressway leading to the fashionable neighborhoods of unincorporated Savannah, calling for information to help solve these murders.

The billboard erected by this wealthy do-gooder completely ignored the 20 homicides occurring between the Wesley Franklin and Rebecca Foley murders, and Savannah didn't even notice. Ford Motor Company noticed, recognizing and rewarding their civic-minded dealer. What troubles me to this day is that there was no backlash about this billboard for its blatantly racist undertone.

I parked my car on the side of President Street and stared at it, wondering how anyone, black or white, could get away with that and not have anyone write a letter to the editor of the newspaper or call in to talk radio to protest. My concern was not shared by the rest of this town. No one said a word, not the black mayor, the black police chief, the black City Manager or the black chairman of the County Commission, who also happened to be president of the Savannah Chapter of the NAACP. No one in the white community of Savannah uttered so much as a syllable of protest, either.

This businessman, so beloved for his commercials with his pet goat, blatantly posted a billboard offering rewards of $20,000 for information in the murders of three white people and completely ignores the 20 black victims murdered in between. But that's how things are when you have money in Savannah-- or Hardeeville, if you have been kicked out of Savannah. Pure poli-tricks.

181

The Shante Cooper case is one that has always troubled me and continues to bother me to this day, mostly because I remember riding Cuyler-Brownsville and passing a makeshift memorial to her that was stapled to a telephone pole at West 38th and Harden Street: a simple photograph and some plastic flowers was all there was to attest to a silent protest and fading memory, a meager offering that remains with me always.

Shante was sitting on a porch when a car came speeding through the neighborhood and an occupant fired one round in the direction of a group of people standing on the corner. The round hit Shante and killed her. Roger Mydell was assigned the case. Few leads were generated; a car, a gunshot, and she was dead. Mydell was a hell of a detective and would go on to serve on the U.S. Marshal Service Fugitive Task Force before being promoted to Sergeant. He ran down every single lead in Shante's case until all were exhausted, but found no answers.

Three years later, Alan Riley, a former County officer working robbery, ran across a kid who was in big trouble. Riley was a real cop, an Old School Detective who had little use for the administration, worked his cases, and liked to be left alone. While executing a search warrant on a house in Clearview occupied by several people, he found a sleeping subject sucking his thumb. A few weeks later there was a robbery of a

182

prostitute in one of the projects and the victim told Riley that the robber did the strangest thing: he was pointing a gun at her and sucking his thumb. Riley put the thumbsucker in a line up and sure enough, he had his suspect in the robbery.

Despite his tender years, this was the young man's third armed robbery conviction, which in Georgia means a potential life sentence. Shortly after locking up the kid, Riley got a letter from jail: the kid had information on a murder and could reveal who was the shooter and where the gun was hidden. Riley confirmed the information and turned it over to homicide. J-Hunt finished the case. He identified a third passenger and they confirmed the information supplied by the informant, and after three years and four months, Shante Cooper's murderer was arrested. Riley wasn't mentioned in the press conference-- nor was he in the audience-- but without him the Cooper case would not have been solved.

But that's Savannah for you: A young mother of three living in a historically impoverished neighborhood is killed in a random act of stupidity and nobody cares. Another young lady from a prominent family and whose godmother was a County Commissioner leaves a dance with friends and goes to a house where marijuana and narcotics are being sold, they are robbed, and the young woman is shot and later dies. Savannah goes berserk and puts City Hall on notice that this is unacceptable.

Today, children play on the fields of the Jennifer Ross Soccer Complex on Sallie Mood Drive at Eisenhower. But there is no field or memorial for Shante Cooper. The Hostess City, with its gross average income of more than $2 billion per year from the tourism industry, has changed in many ways since the days when slavery was the foundation of its economy...or has it?

There has always been crime in Savannah, there will always be crime in Savannah, and anywhere there are people. It's the reason why law enforcement is necessary. When violent crime escalates, Savannahians harken back to the days during the early 1990's, when the Ricky Jivens gang terrorized the town. The mere name Jivens causes long-time residents to shiver. Jivens was an anomaly, a one-time deal that has been done for 25 years but his memory still hangs over the town like moss on the oak trees.

Little Ricky and his ilk taught the rising generation of gangsters not to call themselves a gang, preferring "organization" instead, and taking their name from their neighborhood: The Hitch Village Posse and Carver Village Thoroughbreds. After all, They were smart enough to notice that the local chapters of nationally known gangs like the Crips and Bloods and Gangster Disciples received harsher sentences under RICO statutes, and learned to be a little less conspicuous. Gangs gave up killing for fun and gang initiations, and only killed when deals went sour or there was a territorial dispute. Most gangs followed suit, wised up, saw the errors in their old ways, and found clever ways to disguise themselves: MOB tattoos, which stood for Member of Bloods, was creatively adapted to mean Money Over Bitches, borrowed from a Tupac Shakur song; The GD tat of the Gangster Disciples became Growth & Development, to mean that they were a bunch of community activists and not a criminal enterprise subject to RICO statutes and the federal sentences that came along with them. Perhaps the most clever of all disguises was the CVT that came to mean Christ Versus Thugs, instead of Carver Village Thoroughbreds. I looked at the young man who uttered that one and just shook my head.

Ricky Jivens was in power at the height of the crack cocaine epidemic in Savannah. His arrest as part of a wider crackdown was a major

184

blow to local crime. As time marched on and citizens forgot what it was like to wake up to news of a shooting or two and a murder every week, they became comfortable again and so did the criminals. People who examine how unfair the minimum sentences for drug offenses have forgotten why they were imposed in the first place. Enforcing federal guidelines for offenses involving crack cocaine is now viewed as racist because of the mistaken belief that only minorities use and are affected by the crack problem.

Crack, cocaine, heroin, methamphetamine, OxyContin, morphine, methadone-- none of these narcotics cares anything about race, religion, socioeconomic background; they destroy indiscriminately. What does not change is the violence that exists alongside the business side of them.

The violent crime and homicide rate continues to rise because politics have become more important than justice in Savannah, GA. Law enforcement in 2010 and thereafter has become scrutinized to the point where public trust has been breached. The emphasis that should rightfully be placed on significant criminal activity is being misspent focusing on law enforcement corruption. Instead of focusing on criminals, too much time and energy is being wasted trying to turn administrative miscues into criminal charges, molehills into mountains, misdemeanors into felonies, and state charges into federal offenses.

Crime suppression units like EXPO no longer exist because a kinder and gentler approach to dealing with crime is currently in fashion. Anyone who ever went to kindergarten knows you can have all the rules you want. You can ask nicely and give gentle reminders all day long. But there will always be a small portion of the class that will only understand one thing: harsh discipline. Without that discipline, people get comfortable with bending the rules and breaking the laws. The longer this continues, the worse it will get.

When I was a kid, I pushed limits and was met with discipline. If I blamed a teacher or shirked responsibility for my actions, the discipline was even harsher. Nowadays, teachers are held responsible for children's bad behavior and when discipline is introduced, children are seen as victims. In the streets it is no different. When criminals act up and meet with discipline, the police are the villains and the criminals are the victims.

Of course, there are people in positions of authority that overstep the bounds of effective discipline but they remain the exception, not the rule. I worked on the most aggressive CSU in the history of Savannah Policing and I never saw anyone step over the line when it came to administering discipline. We were taught that there was a line and sometimes we came within an inch of it, but we always toed the line. Crossing that line was and is not acceptable. The respect for the line is why the thin blue line is an honorable profession. Gary Glemboski, Detective Ron Pearson, Sergeant Mike Robbins and the Dauphinee brothers do not tolerate that line being crossed and the tradition lives on.

I can sum up Savannah's crime problem in a few sentences:

Rufus Brown was contacted by violent crime detectives who were looking for a subject thought to be involved in an execution-style triple murder. The victims were put on their knees and shot in the back of the head. Detectives didn't have enough evidence to charge the suspect so they needed to catch him in a position where they would have the leverage to squeeze information out of him. There was no one better to find a subject in such a position than Rufus Brown and, true to form, Brown found the subject in a parked car sitting on a bomb.

As Brown approached, the subject began making furtive movements, an officer safety concern. No stranger to this type of situation, Brown ordered: *My man, put your hands on the steering wheel or you're going to have a bad fucking day.*

The exchange was recorded by an officer equipped with a body camera who was positioned behind Brown. The subject was removed from the vehicle and found to be in possession of felony amounts of narcotics, just the kind of leverage detectives were hoping for, and was turned over for investigation.

The next day Rufus Brown was called into internal affairs for a violation of the department's rudeness policy. I ask the reader: why would any officer risk their life to be treated like that?

*   *   *   *   *

Glen Castro was not a member of EXPO but he was a hell of a street cop, a highly aggressive guy who knew how to gather intelligence on the street and what to do with it. He was assigned to a plain clothes detail in 2015, and positioned in a park where there was a large gathering of teenagers. Castro picked out a young man displaying the characteristics of an armed gunman. Castro spoke to the kid and disarmed him of a street sweeper concealed in his waistband.

This particular weapon was an antique-styled sawed off shotgun with two hammers that needed to be pulled back to fire. The hammers were pulled back when Castro took the gun off the kid. While unloading the weapon it misfired, striking Castro's vehicle but not injuring anyone. It was then that the kid informed Castro that one of the hammers was messed up and the gun could go off at any time. A malfunctioning, prohibited weapon designed to inflict massive damage removed from a kid at a public gathering is a good day's work for any officer, I would say.

A medal? Promotion? Nope, a reprimand and a front-page headline: "Savannah-Chatham Police Officer Accidentally Discharges Sawed-off Shotgun Taken from 15-Year-Old" instead of "Hero cop Disarms Juvenile of Malfunctioning Weapon at Public Gathering."

Sometimes it seems it doesn't pay to go out and save lives anymore.

In 2006, we were allowed to go out and police. In 2017, officers have to look over their shoulder and ask for guidance from supervisors to do anything or they end up with an internal affairs case for not doing their job.

* * * * *

Guns. Firearms. Gats. Burners. Heaters. Tools. Bangers. Straps. Call them whatever you want, but if I had to choose a favorite, I would choose working gun cases. When I was on patrol, finding dope was exciting but nothing matched the adrenaline rush I got when I took a gun off a bad guy. When I was working narcotics, search warrants that landed large amounts of dope were great but nothing was better than finding guns. When I worked on an ATF Task Force, guns were our goal and we got a bunch. During the execution of search warrants and controlled drug buys, guns were what we were after. The goal for me was to remove the guns from the guys that used them on the streets. It is what drove me. I've seen what guns do to people, the blood, the torn flesh, the shattered bones. I've watched as life drained out of a young man's eyes and I've seen people larger than life without any life left in them because a bullet shattered their skull, and what the gas and energy that was transferred from the projectile did to the contents of their head.

A little known fact: I hate guns. I've always been good with one but I hate them. I have qualified Expert every time I tested, in both my military and police careers. Expert marksmanship badges and ribbons for my uniforms, and I've hit everything I aimed at when it mattered, except for a light bulb hanging over a tractor in Baghdad, but that is a story for another time.

During the campaigns for the presidential election in 2016, gun control was a hot button topic. As gun violence plagues cities like Chicago and Savannah, one side calls for a weapon ban while the other side calls for second amendment freedoms to be exercised by every American citizen. Arguments for arming teachers in schools and banning assault rifles are all over social media. The answers to these debates are not easy.

Some people call for tighter restrictions on gun purchases and others call for more laws prohibiting guns, while here in Georgia, we pass laws that say it's okay to carry a gun into a bar.

The one question that I was asked more than any other during my law enforcement career was: *What do you think about carrying concealed?*

I always answered: *I always carry a gun. But remember, you are 110 percent more likely to get shot carrying a gun than if you are not.*

It is never a popular answer. I am asked by young men, old men, young women, old women, married women, single women, men who are drunk, men in the military, college kids, and anyone else who has the time to ask the question. The young guys laugh and shake it off with a bravado and an air that a gun makes them invincible. Other guys look at me hard as if they are challenging me to a duel. Young ladies look at me like, what the hell do you mean?

My explanation is this: Shooting people isn't an easy thing to do. It's an unnatural act. All of my cop and army buddies may cringe but, deep down, they will agree. The best example I can give is from my time in the army, "no shit, there I was":

I was an MP attached to a Cavalry Squadron in Sadr City, Baghdad, Iraq. We were training new Iraqi police officers and were out on Patrol when the Iraqi police reported that one of their officers had been shot. We responded in the same manner and with the same sense of urgency had it been one of our officers.

The suspect was chased into a house. The Iraqi police said he had a pistol and was believed to be carrying a hand grenade. We assembled a squad of soldiers and Iraqi police, and swept the house but couldn't find him. Just as I reached the front yard of the house, I heard a huge commotion and went running back inside. There was a line, a firing squad, for all intents and purposes, in front of me. Five or six soldiers in full battle rattle with M-4 Carbines pointed straight at their target, who was 5-6 yards away. The suspect was behind a small table which had an old iron sewing machine resting on it. Five to six yards away from trained soldiers who were pointing rifles with a maximum effective range of three hundred meters.

190

The suspect had a pistol in his hand but was standing with his arms outstretched like he was tied to a cross. Behind the firing line was a group of Iraqi police officers armed with AK-47 rifles trying to point over the soldiers to get a good line of sight on the suspect. We were training these guys and I, for a short time, felt like we were all on the same side. But I don't care what side you're on, you're not going to point a rifle at the backs of my brothers.

I jumped between the line of soldiers and turned to the Iraqi police and pushed the muzzles of their rifles toward the ceiling so they would not shoot my guys in the back. A loud volley of shots rang out from behind me and it was deafening. The Iraqi police officers had looks of terror on their faces and the room filled with smoke from the discharged cartridges of the 5.56 millimeter rounds. I turned around quickly to see that the suspect was no longer standing and was out of sight. The firing line remained in place but I walked through and jumped over the table and saw the suspect lying in the fetal position, pistol lying near his hand. I kicked it away. And I remember my squad leader yelling, *Dumbass, he might have a grenade!*

Thank God, he didn't, but SSG Joaquin Reyna always had a great way of making a good training point. As I pondered my error, the Iraqi police officers stormed the suspect and yanked him off the ground and whisked him away; their city, their prisoner.

I looked at the floor and there was no blood. I was startled. I looked at the wall where the suspect had been standing and there were no bullet holes. I looked at where the line of Soldiers had been standing and saw spent shell casings on the floor. Then I looked up to find holes in the ceiling. Then I saw a round had dented the old sewing machine.

We returned to the Iraqi police station where the prisoner had been taken and I spoke to one of the interpreters who told me that the suspect had not been hit. Five or six soldiers with highly effective weapons at a range of five to six yards and not a scratch on the target. I pass no judgment and if the reader does, don't. Shooting another human being is an unnatural act. Think whatever you want about what you would do in a similar situation but until you are...keep it to yourself.

I always discourage people who are not well trained from carrying firearms for the simple fact that if you get into a fight, or are the victim of a robbery, or encounter someone who is armed, and you are not prepared to deal with the situation mentally and physically, and you are armed, the armed suspect has no choice but to shoot you because once they find out you are armed they can no longer turn their back on you; you are no longer a victim to them; you are now a threat.

Carrying guns and saving people is not for everyone. There are more laws in this country and in each state to govern how, where and what kinds of guns can be carried than I could possibly list. The laws are in place. What needs to happen to curb gun violence and illegal possession of firearms is to enforce these laws vigorously and to attach penalties to the violation of these laws that are so harsh they will actually serve to deter people from violating the law. Once those penalties are imposed they have to be reinforced with sentences that do not allow for probation or parole. Every thug on the street knows that he does not want to get caught violating the federal gun laws because the penalties are harsh enough where they will do real time. States have only just begun to stop looking the other way and allowing minimum sentences on any violation having to do with guns. It won't solve all the problems, but it is a start.

 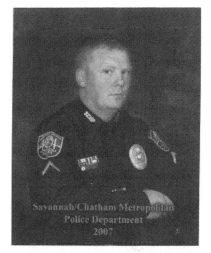

Brand new to the 529th Military Police Company and my glamour shot for Metro.

Lt. John Best and I talking a woman off the Talmedge Bridge.

Rufus Brown and Josh Hunt were the guys that set the tone and pace for EXPO.

K Fraiz, T. Zearing, F. Sawyer, D. Mitchell, L. Baker, R. Smith and me.

Talley and Mitchell conducting a field interview. Tim Lewis and
Terrance Jackson gearing up.

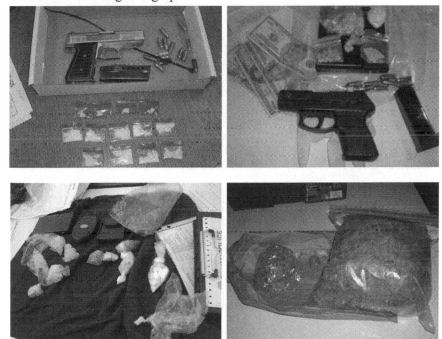

Typical type of arrests EXPO made. The streets of Savannah were safer
when aggressive policing was allowed.

Taking dope off the streets was always a good feeling but nothing compared to getting guns away from the guys who were out using them.

This is the crew that made it happen everyday. A complex group of real police. The kind of guys that make cities safer.

EXPO, NET and K-9 together for Robbery Intervention Detail (RID).
SGT Oglesby is the one with stripes.

Chapter Ten
Lovett or Leave It

Chief Willie Lovett resigned from the Savannah Chatham Metropolitan Police Department in September 2013. He was indicted and convicted on gambling and extortion charges in federal court.

I can't remember the first time I met Chief Lovett, where it was or what it was about. I can, however, tell you how all of the conversations I have ever had with him ended: *Grogan, are people going to prison? Then do it.*

I have no knowledge whatsoever about any gambling or extortion involving Chief Lovett. As a Homicide Detective who had been working law enforcement in Savannah for nine years I was in a singular position to hear about it in a town that loves to talk. What I do have knowledge of is that Willie Lovett was a damn fine cop. In the end, no matter what anyone says, he knew how to police in Savannah, GA.

Whenever there were spikes in crime, Chief Lovett sent his people out to fix it. He did not provide a great deal of instruction on how to do it, he just expected it to get done. If it didn't get done, heads rolled until it did.

Lovett made a name for himself in a community oriented policing platform and ran weed and seed operations because he understood and cared about Savannah. He knew there would always be crime here but he understood that when citizens became uncomfortable and no longer felt safe, that was when it was time for aggressive action. EXPO was a prime example of this dynamic.

After Lovett was convicted of commercial gambling, extortion and making false statements to the FBI, a cry went up to strip Lovett of the pension that he continues to receive for his 40 years of service to the City of Savannah. He earned every dime of that pension and lest we forget, he contributed to that pension fund for those 40 years.

I have spoken to the three men I admire most in law enforcement about the strange case of Willie Lovett and in the end we all agree: like it or not, Willie Lovett knew how to police in Savannah, GA.

Trina Mayes, a former Detective with SCMPD, was indicted, arrested and convicted of making false statements about her relationship with a well-known felon named Rocky Sellers. Trina was mixed up in Chief Lovett's case as the officer with whom he was accused of having an extra-marital affair. I guess the idea was that if Lovett fell, everyone around him should go down, too.

Mayes made statements to Internal Affairs that she did not have a relationship with Sellers while she was a police officer and downplayed her connection to the criminal. Again, I have no knowledge of whether she lied or told the truth or the details of her relationship with Rocky Sellers. I do know, however, that Mayes did not commit a crime. I also am aware that Rocky Sellers had been a criminal since he was 11 years old. Rocky's rap sheet fills a book and yet the district attorney used him as a star witness in the Mayes case.

If what Trina Mayes said in her statements to internal affairs were lies then she should have been fired. Losing a job like hers in this day and age is no small punishment. But to turn it into a criminal charge and a felony, at that?

That is not justice; that's a political agenda.

Chapter Eleven
A Whispered Confession

July 17, 2014 began with a day-long GGIA gang conference that I attended on the heels of having spent the prior three days testifying in my first murder trial as the lead investigator. I got off work, dropped my gun and gear at my house, and went to meet up with my ATF buddies. I made the rounds, spoke to friends, went home.

I was home for a hot minute before my live-in girlfriend and her mother, who was staying with us at the time, got into a heated debate that I wanted no part of so I decided to go out and tank up with gas for a trip I was to make to Fort Stewart the next morning, just to get out of the house. I never made it to the fuel point.

I remember dropping my handheld radio in the car while trying to turn down the volume. Next thing I knew, I was eating the air bag and felt my neck crack from a sudden stop. When I regained my senses I knew this was bad. Not so much the blood from my head and hand, and not so much because of the accident, but I knew I had just pissed away my career.

I got out of the car and saw that I had hit another car from behind and forced it off the road and down an embankment. I rushed to the driver, who was visibly shaken, and asked her why she had stopped; she hadn't. I had driven into the back of her.

She asked me to call the police and I climbed up the hill and back to my car. I called in the accident on my radio and I stood there, thinking about what I had just done. I thanked God that I hadn't seriously injured this young lady. And then I started worrying about the injury to my career.

I grabbed my phone and started calling lawyers. I needed help after a colossal fuck up like this and a lawyer would be the only one who could help me. I never thought I'd be in a position like this, ever.

There I was standing on the side of the Truman Parkway, roughed up, bleeding, and feeling as guilty as I had ever felt about anything. It wasn't so much the fact that I had been drinking that I felt guilty about; it was the fact that I had let down a lot of people and could've seriously injured this woman.

I wish I could tell the reader that this was the first time in my life that I had driven a vehicle under the influence of alcohol but it wasn't. The only difference between this occasion and all the others was the damage to my career.

James Byrne answered my call. He is a good friend and damn fine attorney. But he had also been drinking and could not come to my rescue so he called another old friend, Don Montgomery.

I had known Don since 2005, when he was an Assistant District Attorney in Chatham County, and had recently crossed paths with him when he represented officers who were involved in shootings on the job. No matter the time, weather or situation, Don was always there to help the police. He had been a cop in Baltimore, Maryland, and a damn good one, as I understood it. He worked his way through law school while riding a Beat but gave up police work after sustaining an injury. Don answered the call I wished I never had to make. He told me not to answer any questions until he got there and he was on his way.

I stood on the side of the road for what seemed like an eternity and waited for Don. I spoke to a couple of officers I had known and worked with for years. They checked on me, checked on the woman, called EMS, and did all the things that professional police do.

In the days and months that followed, many people asked me why my boys arrested me, implying that they should have done something to help me.

My response was always: *they did their job.* They did what I and every citizen should have expected them to do. They were there for one reason: I fucked up.

If I didn't do it then, I apologize now for having put them in one of the most uncomfortable and unenviable situations an officer can be placed in by having to arrest another officer, and I admire them for doing their duty.

The details of my trip to the hospital and arrest are still fuzzy. I had a hematoma on top of my head that made me look like a unicorn for about a month. I remember my girlfriend's mom picking me up from jail, which almost caused me to turn around and ask to be held a little longer. Facing my girlfriend was even more difficult. I was her support and stability and I had put her well-being in grave danger. Guilt piled higher than the knot on my head.

The Monday following the accident I went to Internal Affairs for a dreaded but inevitable conversation. I had been placed on administrative leave and officers arrived to take my gun and badge from my house; I am grateful I was not home to see that. Sergeant Robert Larry was the Investigator assigned to my case, another hit because of the great admiration I had for this man.

Robert Larry was a stand-up guy. We had both lost a brother to suicide-- his coming almost a month to the date of my accident-- and having to put him through my trial and tribulation wasn't going to be fun, either; more guilt. I had never worked directly with Sergeant Larry but we had a small circle of friends in common. He was widely respected by detectives in Savannah as one of the most skilled interviewers in our business. And because he is soft spoken I referred to him as "Confession Whisperer".

Larry didn't have to whisper for any confession from me. I went into the interview room and spilled my guts. I told him everything: where I went, who I was with, what I drank and how much, and that I had violated department policy, which is the proverbial nail in the internal affairs coffin.

I was ordered to report to internal affairs for duty while on administrative leave. Unusual because everyone else I had ever known in similar situations was told to stay the hell home. But I was told to come to work and finish case files involving homicides, suicides and aggravated assaults that were still open; cases I had made arrests but had not completed the reports. I tried to convince myself that SCMPD wouldn't be able to get along without me.

I had no issue with finishing my case files. In fact, I intended to drag it out for as long as I could so that I could keep my insurance in order to pay for rehab. Metro was notoriously slow when it came to handing down punishment of its own. Some people I knew stayed on administrative leave for as long as one year while their cases were decided on. Me? I got less than a month.

I went to rehab, then typed files all day until I got a call from Sergeant Larry that he needed to speak to me about a discrepancy in my story.

A discrepancy? A wave of nausea overcame me. The accusation of untruthfulness is the kiss of death for any cop. I thought long and hard about how I was going to handle this. I was compelled to answer questions if I wanted to save my job but at this point, it was abundantly clear to me that I was done at Metro.

I called in sick the next day so I could have more time to decide the best course of action. It boiled down to giving a statement or resigning. If I made any further statement differing so much as a coma from my original statement, it might be misconstrued as being untruthful. Apparently, the issue at hand concerned which vehicle I was driving earlier in the evening of the accident: In my original statement I said that I had been driving my personal vehicle; it was obvious which vehicle I was in when I wrecked. It appeared to me that no matter what else I might say at this point, I wasn't going to save my job. However, I could preserve my career by resigning and taking another position with one of two Chiefs in other jurisdictions that I had already contacted.

I resigned from SCMPD on August 19, 2014.

I would like to say that I moved on, found work in my chosen profession, and got back to doing what I love most: policing. But that is not the case.

In January 2015, I caught wind of the District Attorney's Office looking into my case and was considering handing down an indictment for making false statements about which car I was driving before the accident occurred. Perhaps there was a discrepancy, but it was not a lie. Neither was a discrepancy criminal, lacking criminal intent. Last but not least, I had served the City of Savannah for almost 7 years during which I put some of the worst criminals in prison, broke a few of my fingers, pulled many a muscle, removed guns from the streets, held crying children and a few crying mothers, stood toe to toe with the criminal element, having sacrificed my family and part of my sanity.

Charge me with being a liar? Fuck you.

I told myself that this could not possibly be happening. It would be positively insane for the district attorney to criminally accuse me of making false statements when I still had a long list of murder trials and aggravated assault cases where the DA needed me as a witness.

But in April, insanity came knocking: James Byrne called to say that Assistant District Attorney Christy Barker informed him that she was presenting my case to the Grand Jury. They had done it.

Here I had resigned to avoid even the hint of untruthfulness. I moved out of Chatham County. I went to rehab and hadn't had a drink since the date of my accident. I had started a small business and went back to school to work on my master's degree. I don't know what else I could've done to rehabilitate myself and get back on track.

But the Chatham County District Attorney's Office wanted more. They decided to prosecute me under the auspices of a police Corruption Task Force designed to flush out dirty cops. A DUI on my own time and the DA files it under police corruption. But it just so happens that this action came down on the exact same day-- January 12, 2015-- that attorneys for Sergeant Malik Khaalis filed a selective prosecution motion claiming that the District Attorney's Office was only prosecuting black police officers. The District Attorney's Office put in a request for my case 179 days after the date of the accident. This was no coincidence.

What started out as a strange case only got stranger: An Effingham County Sheriff's Deputy knocked on my door and handed me a subpoena from the Chatham County District Attorney's Office but I was not named as the defendant in the action. I was to appear as a witness in the State's case against Rodderick Jackson.

I called James Byrne and told him about the subpoena. Having retained legal counsel, the DA's office was not to contact me nor I them unless it went through my attorney. Service of the subpoena was followed up by a telephone call from the Assistant DA handling the Jackson case, also a no-no. But this DA's office was rather selective about which rules were followed and which rules were ignored.

James Byrne sent notice to District Attorney Meg Heap that any and all correspondence with me should go through his office. I continued to be contacted by assistant district attorneys who had no idea that I had been indicted nor were they aware that I was on a no-contact list. Yet, they still needed me in court. Not just to show up but to actually testify for the prosecution.

It seems, therefore, that the District Attorney still thought I was a credible witness despite having accused me of being a felonious liar.

Read that last sentence as many times as it takes for the hypocrisy to sink in. Then imagine the ultimate conflict it created in me: I was not torn out of any loyalty to the DA's office; I was torn out of a sense of duty to all the victims who still had open cases in the courts and without my testimony, justice would not be served.

I was torn because of Ellen Scott. I was torn because of Rashaad Spann and his mother Shanell Bryan. I was torn because of Miss Gonzalez. I was even more torn because of Gwendoline Jefferson, mother of Ardearrian, the only homicide victim whose case had not ended with an arrest.

The District Attorney needed me on the witness stand.

I wanted to be on that witness stand.

But it was left to my attorney to forbid it. Not if the same DA who held me up as credible witness in their cases called me a liar in mine.

Chapter Twelve
Mother Teresa Jump the Gun

The first inclination I had that the District Attorney's Office might come after me was so subtle that it almost failed to register. I had been subpoenaed to testify in a murder case on January 12, 2015. The murder occurred on St. Patrick's Day 2013, involving a father killed by his son. I was lead detective in this case and Frank Pennington was the Assistant DA assigned to handle the prosecution.

I liked and admired Frank. His mother was a retired Major from Metro and was later Chief of police in a small municipality in Chatham County. The Major had raised up a hard nosed, intelligent and dedicated prosecutor.

The first day of the trial was jury selection and not much else went on. As we were preparing for court the next day, Frank asked me about my DUI and we talked about the best way to handle it. I suggested that we come right out and tell the jury about it, as if I had nothing to hide. Frank agreed that was the best strategy, but then he asked me something that made me wonder:

It is just the DUI, right?

Yeah, I said. But the question bothered me. I thought: *Does Frank know something I don't?* But we had already been through one murder trial together and I trusted him. When I testified, I explained to the jury why I was no longer with the police department and I testified as to the facts of the case. The defendant pleaded to manslaughter halfway through the trial.

His mother, a key witness, was forced to testify against her son for the murder of her husband. Watching that poor woman divide her loyalty among the ones she loved most was pure torture for me. The plea was the right thing to do if all it did was ease her pain. No one should have to go through that.

On that very same day my troubles were just beginning in another courtroom not too far away when Mike Schiavone filed a motion of selective prosecution on behalf of his client, Malik Khaalis. Schiavone, whom I had immense respect for then and now, called out the District Attorney for only prosecuting black police officers-- Willie Lovett, Trina Mayes and Malik Khaalis-- and for offenses they had never prosecuted before. Christy Barker wasted no time putting in a request for files from Internal Affairs.

Rumor has it that Frank Pennington and Jerry Rothschild were asked for their input whether I should be prosecuted. Jerry's response was to recuse himself from my case due to our friendship.

And of all the cases that went to Assistant DA Barker, mine was the only one selected for prosecution.

How's that for selective?

In July 2015, after having been indicted in April, I was subpoenaed to testify in an aggravated assault case: A woman sipping lemonade while reading a book on the fenced-in patio of her retirement home was shot by two young men when they jumped her fence to rob her. I don't think the suspect meant to pull the trigger but the gun went off as he went over the fence and the bullet struck the victim in the back. He was caught a few blocks away with the gun that matched the shell casing and recovered projectile from the scene.

The suspect decided he would represent himself in court. There is that old saying, he who represents himself has a fool for a client. Aware of the old adage, I sought my attorney's counsel about my testimony in this case and he advised that I should plead the Fifth Amendment to protect against self-incrimination under cross-examination.

This suggestion bothered me because it was the first time I felt like a criminal. My name and likeness had been plastered on the front page of the newspaper when I was arrested, and again when I was indicted, but this was the first action requiring me to defend myself. After having testified in hundreds of cases, I was now going to take the stand in a case I cared deeply about and now, because of this mess, I was going to have to invoke my rights and potentially risk the defendant walking away.

How the hell did a DUI turn into not testifying in another case where an innocent victim was shot?

My attorney explained that if I testified, I opened myself up to having to answer questions that would basically convict me of the DUI, and his feelings were strong that the DA's case against me was weak. Although I wholeheartedly admitted my wrongdoing, the prosecution still had to prove it. I labored with this dilemma for a long time before deciding to go with advice of counsel. It was now time to call the DA's hand.

To put it plainly, I was indicted because the district attorney's office needed a white police officer to prosecute along with all of the black officers already on the firing line. I was indicted on charges that have never

211

been levied against any officer in the history of Savannah police or any other citizen in a DUI case.

The kicker is that the district attorney tried to pull off this stunt under the guise of police corruption. Hence, the tampering with evidence charge that was tacked on.

Lovett, Mayes and Khaalis were all accused of lying about investigations dealing with their conduct as police officers. My case was about a drunk guy driving a car while off-duty. The only connection to my profession was that I was in my unmarked unit at the time of the wreck.

Regardless, I honored the subpoena, primarily because the fool who represented himself didn't realize the opportunity he had to discredit the lead witness in the case. Even with all that, the DA's Office argued that because I was the key witness I was not entitled to my Fifth Amendment protections.

Apparently, in Chatham County, it is the opinion of the district attorney's office that a police officer is not a citizen.

The Chief Superior Court Judge disagreed with the DA's position and ordered that I could not be compelled to testify and that my constitutional protections were solidly in place.

But the assistant district attorney was not done: I was offered a use immunity, which effectively meant that the State could not use my statements against me. I accepted and I testified and the suspect was convicted.

News reporters were all over it, demanding to know how the district attorney could charge me with being a liar but still trusted my credibility enough to testify in their prosecutions.

You can't have it both ways, James Byrne said. *Grogan is either a liar, as they think he is, or he's not. What they did was very short-sighted: They arrested him on trumped up charges, for political reasons, in my opinion, to show how fair they are in prosecuting police officers. The Malik Khaalis case is what we are talking about. There is nothing to them. We'll prove that in court. In the meantime, Grogan is not testifying at any of these.*

The District Attorney responded by filing a motion for a gag order to keep my attorney from exposing any more of their hypocrisy.

The motion was denied.

Apparently, the First Amendment was still in effect in Chatham County even if the Fifth was under attack.

The reader may have noticed that I have gone to great lengths in avoiding race to describe anyone in this book. I did this intentionally in order to make certain strong statements regarding race when it matters and have avoided it at all cost when it doesn't.

There is one point I want to make emphatically clear:

In July 2015, I was granted immunity to testify in a case involving a white woman victim. Thirty days later, I went through the same process in a case involving a black male victim, a case that pulled at my heart more than usual.

I received a call from Shanell Bryan, the mother of a murder victim in a case I worked in February 2014. Ms. Bryan had been told that the DA was considering pleading the case out because I was not going to testify. She wanted to know what was going on with me.

My stomach flipped. I did not know what to say. The only thing I knew to do was be upfront and keep it real. I told her what I had done and what the district attorney said I did. I told her why it made testifying a problem for me. I'm figuring at the same time that this woman was going to say she didn't care about me or about the DA's political agenda. I fully expected her to hate me for not testifying against her son's killer; I got the exact opposite.

Ms. Bryan told me that she knew all about my DUI case, said it had been all the talk of her criminal justice class. She was well aware that the district attorney's office was pursuing my case only because I was white. She told me that all she wanted was for her son's case to be over. In the end, she said, no matter what happened to the other young man who killed her son, her son was still gone.

I was stunned by her compassion for my plight and for her thoughtfulness. I told her that if she wanted me to testify, immunity or no, I would do it.

Ms. Bryan told me to follow my attorney's advice-- she had learned at least that much in her criminal justice class-- and she told me, more importantly, to do what was best for me and my family.

I will be forever grateful to Shanell Bryan for her kindness; strong woman.

* * * * *

A hearing was held a day or two later where I notified the district attorney that I would be pleading the Fifth. The Judge presiding over this case concurred with the Chief Superior Court Judge in the previous case that my protection against self-incrimination still applied and I could not be compelled to testify.

The stark difference in this case was that the assistant district attorney offered no immunity and instead allowed the defendant to plead to the lesser offense of manslaughter. The defendant had never been in any trouble so his sentence would be drastically reduced. The other stark difference in this case was that the victim was a young black man.

The assistant DA who made the plea agreement told the Judge and the *Savannah Morning News* that the deal was made because "Grogan refused to testify". And of all the things that I have ever read about me in the press, this is the one comment that made me angriest.

The facts in this case were simple: two young men were arguing over a girl. One of the young men left his job, got a ride home, picked up his brother and got his gun, and went to where he knew his rival to be. The suspect admitted to fighting with his victim for a moment and then a gun went off. The suspect lied about having a gun but when confronted with the fact that the victim's gun had not been fired-- and the victim had been shot in the back of the head-- the suspect admitted to bringing and firing and disposing of his own gun.

I have never claimed to be the best detective of all time, but this was a case of clear-cut murder.

Granting immunity in the case of a white female victim and not granting immunity in the case of a black male victim is racist.

*   *   *   *   *

I knew Meg Heap as an assistant district attorney and I had respect for her. She came to our roll call and answered questions about Fourth Amendment issues. She told us when we could search and when we couldn't; when detaining suspects was justified; and suggestions on how to keep suspects talking when they were not in custody.

When Heap ran for district attorney she ran on the platform that she would repair the breach in the relationship between the DA's office and the police department. She has, in my opinion, an inability to make difficult decisions and uses the Grand Jury as a crutch: "It wasn't my decision but the Grand Jury has spoken".

Anyone who has worked in law enforcement knows an indictment is an easy thing to get. You can indict a ham sandwich, as they like to say in defense counsel circles. A Grand Jury basically hears a one-sided presentation of facts, as laid out by the district attorney. If a prosecutor is doing their job and the investigator presents all the facts, the system works just fine. But when evidence that doesn't help the prosecution is withheld, then the system falters, especially if political agendas are the driving force.

Meg Heap became a master of deferring decisions to Grand Juries under the guise of remaining "impartial". She pulled that maneuver in the case of an officer-involved shooting and again in the strange case of Tony Thomas, a controversial City Councilman, who was accused of inappropriate relationships with young men and drug use.

District Attorney Heap sent the Thomas case to the Grand Jury only to have it returned as a no bill because the alleged violations were outside the statute of limitations. It isn't a judgment call; it's decreed by law. If the district attorney knew these violations were outside the statute of limitations and still presented to the Grand Jury, she wasted time and money, not to mention the costs to the County.

On the other hand, if the district attorney was not aware of the statute of limitations, she should have been, and in that case it is sheer incompetence.

In my opinion, I truly believe that Meg Heap would rather be viewed by the public as incompetent than to be on the wrong side of a political battle. Tony Thomas is one of the most despised officials in Savannah City government-- but he's still a Councilman-- and rather than simply telling her constituents that the allegations brought against him were outside the statute of limitations, she instead chose to lean on the Grand Jury and have them make the decision so she could say she did all she could.

This is a pattern of cowardice that Heap's office had shown since her election. When she was elected in 2012, gangs were the big news in Savannah and their prosecution was a fashionable political agenda. In November 2012, there was a shooting at the Coastal Empire Fair when two rival gangs decided to have a showdown in the middle of a crowd of thousands of funseekers. Tatumville and Hellhole were identified as participants. SCMPD had little to no current intel on these gangs even though they had been identified as early as 2005, which put Violent Crimes Detectives in a hole from the start and behind the power curve when the investigation began.

I know this to be true because I was in the office when it all went down.

Arrests were made but mostly on weak false statements. The district attorney's office picked up the charge and came to violent crimes detectives with an affidavit to conduct several search warrants on gang members. Nowhere could an affiant be found to provide a sworn statement and none of the detectives were comfortable with the factual basis. They ended up assigning the gang investigator to be the affiant, the first search warrant he had been the affiant in the ten years I had known him.

Of greater concern to detectives was that Lenard Mikell was no-billed in a Grand Jury on a murder charge. Mikell was found to be the shooter in the killing of Tiyates Franklin, who was gunned down during a confrontation on River Street on Labor Day, shortly before the Fairground battle. According to the district attorney, this murder was also linked to the war between Hellhole and Tatumville. The Grand Jury decided that there was not enough probable cause to pursue the Murder charge against Mikell, who ended up testifying against gang members in the prosecutions that followed.

In 2013, the district attorney's agenda was gangs; in 2014, it was police corruption. Lenard Mikell walked on a murder charge in order to further a gang prosecution. In 2015, Fashaad Kennedy was allowed to plead to manslaughter in order to further a trumped up police corruption

218

charge. Considering the foregoing, it seems to me that Meg Heap will ignore what is in the best interest of justice to further her political agenda.

I only hope Savannah remembers this around election time.

Sadly, I lost respect for Ms. Heap and her Chief Assistant Greg McConnell long before my case. Ms. Heap's campaign promise to bring her office back together with the police department in a new spirit of trust and cooperation was never achieved or even attempted, for that matter. The best example I can provide to show up her campaign promise involved the beating of an off-duty police Sergeant by a motorcycle gang in 2013. At a time when gangs were still a hot button issue for Ms. Heap, a support club for Hells Angels was starting up locally.

The sergeant was downtown drinking with his buddies and was walking down West Congress Street in the heart of Savannah's City Market. Passing the entrance to a club he bumped into a young man wearing his motorcycle club's cut. The biker and his pals took exception and, as City of Savannah cameras recorded, the officer was surrounded by five guys, punched from behind, pushed against a wall and beaten. An on-duty detective broke up the fray.

I was assigned the case and interviewed members of the motorcycle club who told me the victim had bumped into their club president. I took their statements and identified the structure of the club and who held what position. I viewed the video and was able to identify the individuals that took part in the assault. But I was discouraged from pursuing the gang angle by my supervisor, who said we have never had a problem with these guys before. So the case was held up until I could follow up, hoping maybe these guys would find other trouble to get into.

The pace of the homicide office, however, made it difficult to get back around to this motorcycle club. Turns out they stayed out of harm's way and the club folded when they failed to gain a foothold in Savannah. After all, Georgia is Outlaw country and they weren't about to let a Hells Angel support club grow on their turf.

Nonetheless, these punks beat up one of our guys and broke his ribs and that's not something we forget. Not me, anyway. When I was moved to the gang unit, I took their file with me, along with the video and everything else I needed for a successful prosecution. I delivered the package to the DA's office and spoke directly to Ms. Heap about the case.

The case was never prosecuted.

The motorcycle club and all its members were white. The victim was a police officer.

I had seen Ms. Heap's office drop murder charges against a young man in exchange for his testimony against two gangs where all members were black, even though there was notably little intelligence on the structure of the gang. Here I had presented the structure of the motorcycle club and a video of their assault of a police officer and, to this day, they have not been prosecuted.

I've thought about this case a lot. But since I continue to be subpoenaed almost monthly to testify in other cases, the reason they don't prosecute the motorcycle club can't be because they don't think I'm a credible witness. In my opinion, the only difference in this case is the race of the suspects. That, and the absence of media coverage compelling the district attorney to take action.

Chapter Thirteen
Is Savannah Safe?

I've been asked that question many times. Over the years I have noticed that I tend to give the same answers to the same questions. When I am asked if Savannah is safe, I always say: If you're not smoking, selling or trying to buy crack, your chances of getting shot in Savannah are pretty slim.

For clarification, substitute any illicit substance for "crack" and it works equally well. I have rarely worked or seen a case where a victim was truly innocent of any and all wrongdoing in a situation which led to them being shot. That's not to say that there is no such thing as an innocent victim: Shante Cooper is a perfect example. She was doing nothing wrong and more importantly, she was doing nothing to contribute directly or indirectly to her death. Unless sitting on your porch and talking to neighbors is a contributing factor.

The same cannot be said for Jennifer Ross, however. In all honesty, I have no idea what Miss Ross was doing in Orleans Square at 3 o'clock in the morning. I know this much: After attending a dance, she went back to a friend's house where two of her companions were dealing drugs. And the thing about drugs is that no matter what, drugs eventually attract trouble, which is why they have been made illegal.

I have seen drugs destroy lives. I have seen people addicted to drugs do things that they would not ordinarily do in their sober mind, like rob, steal, rape and even kill while under the influence or in an attempt to score more dope. I have also spent the majority of my career investigating those who prey upon and capitalize on addiction. I made the focus of my career catching the guys who profit from drugs. The guys who prey on addicts and rob suppliers in order to better supply their customers.

If a dealer can rob a weaker dealer and sell the harvest they have stolen, and make a profit without any real cost involved, they will do it and call it smart business.

The truly evil criminals I have known think nothing about what supplying dope does to the person who depends on it or their family. They do not concern themselves with the potential hazard they present to the victims they rob or catch slipping. They are indifferent to the hazards their lifestyle presents to them.

I have heard endless arguments about the legalization of drugs to which I also have but one response: Anyone who is for the legalization of drugs-- including marijuana-- is either themselves a drug user or have never seen someone who is.

Narcotics create a subculture that will do most anything to circumvent conventional or legal means to get what they want. It happens on college campuses, in inner cities, on golf courses, and in city halls all over America. Some people never experience the true pitfalls of narcotics and these subcultures. Some people are lucky enough to enjoy a night of altered consciousness and wake the next day with a hangover or lost wallet. For some that is the worst consequence for their misbehavior. Other people end up in situations due to their altered mindset that they would most likely never encounter in their right minds: fights, wrecks and arrests. St. Patrick's Day in Savannah is a perfect illustration of this.

222

Chapter Fourteen
Every Cop Is A Criminal and All the Sinners Saints

Savannah had 28 murders in 2006, down from 37 in 2005. Violent crime as a whole was down 15.2 percent, primarily because SCMPD was allowed to police.

Greg Capers, Rufus Brown, Josh Hunt, Terrance Jackson, Floyd Sawyer, Lorenza Baker, Kelvin Frazier, Tim Lewis, Antonio McBride, Terry Zearing, Darren Mitchell, Jeron Young, Chris Talley, David Brand, Jeff Oliver, Randy Veal, Randy Smith, Fred Hill and Randy Powell went out at all hours of the day and night and dealt with everything Savannah has to offer. They did so at their own peril, not only physically but mentally, emotionally and even spiritually.

There are ethical dilemmas that officers go through about who should be arrested and who shouldn't, and the drastic effect the arrest potentially has on a person's life. These officers go where no one else wants to go. When we rolled into a neighborhood, we didn't stop the little old lady who wasn't wearing a seatbelt. We went after the guys hanging on the street corner at midnight or high noon. We stopped and found out what they were doing, and if they weren't doing anything, we said goodbye and kept looking for the ones that were. Sometimes we shook hands or gave dap-hugs to guys we had built a rapport with. They knew what our job was about and we knew what they were doing. But if we didn't catch them at it, we treated them like any other law abiding citizen. If they gave us shit, we handed it back. We were the guys you wanted to see when things went bad and in Savannah, there is always something bad going down somewhere.

I ran into one of my best informants in 2012, and he asked me a riveting question:

Why don't y'all police anymore?

I do, I said. *I'm just sneakier about it than I used to be.*

So the Blue and Whites don't jump out like they used to, he pressed. 'Cause those boys just roll right past like we ain't doin' shit.

I did not know how to respond but it made me think: our police aren't allowed to do what EXPO, NET, DSO, TRAP and other crime suppression units were allowed to do. The magnifying glass has been aimed directly at police response to any given situation and not on the person committing the crime. The criminal has an instant appeal process by calling and complaining.

It used to be that a complaint was registered and directed to the supervisor and they would handle it unless it was a serious offense warranting the attention of internal affairs. Nowadays all complaints go straight to the Officer of Professional Standards in internal affairs and has an instant effect on the officer's personnel file, whether the complaint is substantiated or not.

My favorite quote from Toby Taylor, is: we have developed an infraction mindset in a felony world. The reader has probably heard it referred to as The Ferguson Effect, where officers ride their calls but when it comes to approaching suspects of wrongdoing, they will stop and think about the repercussions and choose the path of least resistance.

The Savannah Chatham Metropolitan Police Department has an old saying: No one ever gets fired for doing nothing.

In all my time with the department, I never believed that but it has become the undeniable truth in 2017.

* * * * *

No matter how much attention a murder may get from the media or how much pressure rains down from city hall or even the command staff, I've only seen murder cases worked one way: tirelessly. I've seen detectives work to the point where they could no longer hold a pen. I've ridden in cars with guys who made turns onto streets that weren't real because they were checking one last lead before they took a break. I've worked until I literally couldn't think of one more thing I could possibly do to figure out another angle or possibility that might help my investigation.

None of that was ever influenced by the race, gender, or religion of the victim.

I worked five murders as the primary Investigator, assisted in approximately sixty other murder investigations, either directly or indirectly, all in less than two years of my assignment to homicide. I've worked alongside white detectives and black detectives, young and old, male and female, and I never saw one case worked differently because of race or gender or religion.

The dedication I witnessed by the detectives working these cases is difficult to put into words. I can state without hesitation that I have been awe struck watching how detectives worked their cases. That is not to say all because there are detectives with different capabilities, but the ones who are truly meant to do the job do so in an amazing fashion. I've spoken to everyone I know that ever worked a homicide and almost all agree that in their experience not once have they seen a case worked a different way for any reason dealing with race.

That said, how the media portrays a murder or the importance of one case over another is an entirely different story. Whenever news stations or politicians get involved, there is an entirely different spin on what gets done. When Shante Cooper was killed in an errant drive-by shooting, police officers and homicide detectives worked the case until every lead was exhausted. It took years but good police work eventually turned up the evidence to convict Rodney Simmons of her murder.

But it wasn't until the Cooper case was solved that it received any media coverage or community response.

When Jennifer Ross was shot and her companions robbed after leaving an apartment where narcotics were being distributed, police officers and robbery detectives responded and immediately started running down leads. And when Ms. Ross succumbed to her injuries, homicide detectives took up the charge. The media went wild and members of her prominent family put the pressure on city hall, calling for action. County Commissioners closely followed the case and when the suspects were put on trial, Court TV covered it gavel to gavel.

Two ends of the media spectrum but no difference whatsoever in the manner in which both cases were investigated.

226

* * * * *

Murders get worked how they get worked, I like to say. Sometimes the detective is blessed to have all the information that is needed from the jump and with others it's almost like the victim fell out of an unidentified flying object.

Sometimes we followed a lead to its obvious conclusion while at other times we chased down a hundred rabbit holes and found nothing but carrot shit. Eyewitnesses see everything; sometimes they can describe every detail of what happened and sometimes they develop selective amnesia; sometimes they lie outright to throw off the detective and some witnesses lie purely for the dramatic effect.

Some cases get worked by detectives who are new to The Game, some get worked by old pros beaten down and tired from years of working murders, but they all get worked.

No one wants to be the detective with their name in red on an open homicide. Open homicides are worse than a gunshot wound to a detective. I have one red letter case that keeps me up nights all these years later.

Murder is the ultimate case around the clubhouse but calls for service are not much different. Officers ride their beats and respond to calls to make a difference in this tired old world. They do not ride slower to get to one neighborhood as opposed to any other. police, however, are like any other profession and some are more skilled than others. Some are good at their job and some are not so good. But the suggestion that the level of service or response time differs based on the race of the victim or even the race of the officer offends me to my core.

227

I have never met an officer who was dispatched to an emergency and stopped to ask what was the victim's race. Police respond and are on the scene to help. Now that the national spotlight is trained on police, it has become common practice to pull the race card and the mainstream media would have us believe that racist police officers seek targets to violate and that it's all based on a racial agenda. From the moment the Michael Brown and Eric Gardner and Freddie Gray and Alton Sterling incidents occurred, they captured headlines even before the basic facts had been established and without a single thought as to whether information was accurate and complete.

This is precisely the reason why criminal cases are tried in courtrooms and not on street corners by lynch mobs.

American jurisprudence is based on the concept that facts of a case have to be fully established before judgment can be made. The media operates by a much weaker standard and cares little if the erroneous information disseminated over the airwaves and across headlines subverts justice as long as their political agenda remains intact. The media once upon a time understood that they had a sacred duty not to foment hatred and fear that created a divide between the races and classes; truth mattered. But in this current climate, if it bleeds it leads and facts exist only to fan the flames of emotional response.

There once was a marked difference between The New York Times and The National Enquirer, but I can't tell one from the other these days purely reading their headlines.

"Hands Up, Don't Shoot!" became the hottest slogan in America since "Where's the beef?" People took to the streets in protest and it became a popular fad to hate the police. Through it all officers have continued to respond to thousands of emergencies each and every day, saved lives, and made the streets safer for all. The rest of America suddenly became experts in law enforcement instantly based on what they had seen on TV. The situation devolved to the inexpressibly tragic point where police Offices have been murdered in the street while performing their duties.

The media refrains from reporting on the race of cop killers nor do they hold an entire ethnic group or religion responsible for the actions of a few. But the media thinks nothing at all about holding all police officers responsible for the actions of a few who get caught up in these instant national tragedies, even when the actions are justified.

Some police chiefs and sheriffs have rightfully stood by their personnel and come to their defense while others have caved to the pressure of their employers. I can think of no other profession that is under the type of scrutiny that dogs law enforcement. I can think of no other profession where people glimpse segments of a video, have no idea of what the given situation is, and have never once responded to a scene where they might have to make sudden life or death decisions, and still think they are qualified to speak or critique. Some of these decisions made by officers are made in mere seconds, sometimes when they are scared, and sometimes when the facts and circumstances are completely unknown.

While other professions are commonly criticized-- doctors and lawyers and athletes-- none involve life and death situations where split decisions must be made to the extent that it happens in Law Enforcement. Yet all it takes to be heard on how police should best handle situations is a cell phone and a Twitter account. Put it on Facebook and it becomes instant fact. Give the news media a video and they'll run with it even before they know what the scene depicts.

True or false, city governments are now bowing to public pressure and police Departments are forced in the name of transparency to turn over names and photographs of officers so that they can be hunted and their families placed in danger.

Tell me what salary is worth that type of scrutiny?

Officers indicted on trumped up charges to appease the hysteria created by stories that have no factual basis, their lives forever changed and careers gone forever because of baseless accusations.

The thing I can't get past when I see all this anti-police rhetoric is the sheer audacity of people who think they can come to a conclusion based on segments of a recording that captures fragments of a situation and without the benefit of police training. For every situation I was ever involved in, my reactions were based on extensive training and even greater extensive experience. I know first-hand that no situation can or should be handled one set way. Sometimes even I judge an officer's actions from the segmented videos I see broadcast over media.

The difference with me though, other than training and experience, is I keep my opinion to myself. I do not dare pretend to know what the officer in question should have done or what I would have done in these same circumstances. I try to take the approach that I was not there and did not see, hear, smell, feel or know what the officer knew at the time of the incident. One thing I know for sure is that in this day and age the media will not provide us with the whole and unbiased circumstances so

230

that the viewer can arrive at an educated decision. This has been proven time and again since the tragedy in Ferguson, Missouri.

Journalism in America is dead. Sex and scandal sell papers. As Mick Jagger says, *Every cop is a criminal and all the sinners saints*. The problem with social media is the average person is only beginning to understand how powerful their opinion is. Hell, you don't even have to use your real name on these accounts. It wasn't long ago when those who wanted to be heard had to identify themselves and if they wanted to address the masses had to do so in the presence of others. Sure, opinions could be expressed but they were subject to criticism and debate. It took courage to say things that were controversial or inflammatory because the speaker could be challenged. But with the world's current obsession with social media, anyone can say anything in complete anonymity and without accountability or repercussion.

I've looked into the numbers and I see where all this is going. Savannah, like many other cities, suffers from this Ferguson Effect. Looking at statistics from 2005 until 2015 shows a drastic decline in the number of arrests of 46 percent and an increase from 37 homicides in 2005 to 58 murders in 2015.

There was an immediate 24 percent decrease in homicides the year that EXPO was in existence, which had residual effects in the two years that followed when, coincidentally, Operation Raging Waters was being conducted.

Michael Brown was shot by Officer Darrin Wilson in Ferguson, Missouri, in August 2014 and the national outrage that followed has turned into American lore but the ripple effects are still being felt in Savannah. In

2014, SCMPD made only 9,933 arrests compared to 12,333 the year before. The rate dropped further to 8,411 in 2015. Now compare these numbers to the number of arrests the year that EXPO was in business: 15,524. The decrease is significant.

The decrease in arrests is directly tied to the increase in the number of murders in Savannah: In 2014 there were 33 murders; in 2015, there were 58; and 2016 hit the 50 mark again. These are the facts and they are not disputed.

I consciously chose not to crunch the violent crime stats because they have been historically padded for political reasons, especially during elections. Felonies are downgraded to misdemeanors and many misdemeanors go unreported or cut loose. But there is no denying that the downward trend in the number of arrests has created an upwards trend in the number of murders.

My truest and most heartfelt admiration goes out to all the rookies who have answered the call to protect and serve that has been overwhelmed by all the negative media attention, the ones who in the face of this constant accusation that all police are racist and need to be dealt with, still sign up, still train and still take an oath to take care of communities that will turn on them the second the use of force on somebody's child occurs.

To subject themselves to all that for a meager $38,000 a year amazes me and I salute them.

I did my duty and Savannah was a safer city while I worked for SCMPD.

I am an alcoholic who made a stupid mistake that I will forever regret.

I was rightfully prosecuted for driving under the influence because I did just that.

I was wrongfully accused of false statements and tampering with evidence because I am a white male.

But I was wrongfully prosecuted because I was a police officer.

Chapter Fifteen
Sleepy Time Down South

2017 got off to a bad start with a call from my attorney James Byrne. James never called with good news and he wasn't calling to wish me a happy new year. The purpose of his call was to inform me that he was leaving private practice to take a job in the public sector that would create a conflict in his continuing to represent me. James had been with me from the start of my case, no doubt, because we are friends. He did not call to cut me loose; he called with a solution: he had already enlisted the help of his friend and mentor Mike Schiavone to take my case.

"Iron Mike" Schiavone is arguably Savannah's finest criminal defense attorney. He represented Sharron "Nikki" Redmond in the Miss Savannah Murder case and won an acquittal after presenting a self-defense argument. Few people knew the whole and true story of this case but Schiavone's defense of Redmond was brilliant and moreover it was absolutely correct.

One thing about Mike Schiavone is that he had always done the right thing in the courtroom and never resorts to lies in order to prevail. He had stepped in for James Byrne when the DA's office attempted to take advantage of Byrne being tied up in a murder trial by trying to put me in jail after having been indicted. Schiavone also stepped up during the DA's failed attempt at imposing a gag order on Byrne. Mike is a good guy; he is an even better lawyer.

Two weeks prior to trial Schiavone and I went over what we needed for discovery: medical records and a list of witnesses. I gathered as much information as I could and listed the people I thought would help my case. I went to my doctor's office and retrieved his report containing information in strong support of my defense. I included Dr. Jon Odom on the witness list and also suggested that we include Karl Knoche, Assistant United States Attorney, whom I had known for years and offered to be a character witness in my trial.

Mr. Schiavone, in due course, filed the information with the court and copied the district attorney's office. He promptly received a telephone call from Jim Durham in the U.S. attorney's office saying that they had been contacted by Assistant District Attorney Christy Barker, who explained that I had been offered a reckless driving plea early on and that I had turned it down, with the implication that I was seeking some sort of media attention. This, of course, was inconsistent with the information I had given Karl Knoche.

This maneuver by Barker created a conflict and was of great concern to Knoche because I had failed to mention any reckless driving offer, the reason being, it was never offered. While it had been my hope and dream from the beginning of this case to get the charges reduced to reckless driving-- allowing me to pay a fine and get back to police work— the offer was not forthcoming. Even my attorney, James Byrne, considered the reduction of a DUI to reckless driving to be a major win, and James is an expert DUI lawyer.

Then I received word that Barker had also contacted Dr. Odom and told him a similar story. What concerned me most about this maneuver was wondering why my character witness and material witness needed to know anything about plea negotiations that never took place.

The only answer I could come up with is that Barker was making every attempt to influence my witnesses from testifying on my behalf.

Heading into trial I had an effectively clear picture of what the DA's approach was going to be and by tampering with my witnesses I knew that they were prepared to go to any depths in order to win.

As part of my discovery we offered as evidence of my good character a list of commendations I had been awarded for military service and my law enforcement career, along with the list of witnesses and the doctor's report detailing the head injury I sustained during the accident. All of this is generally considered to be part of discovery.

However, the DA's Office immediately filed a motion to keep all of it out of court: my witnesses, commendations-- even the medical report—were to be suppressed. At the hearing on the motion to suppress Judge Walmsley denied every motion James Byrne made and signed off on it. And at this point I had a terrible feeling that the Judge was neither fair nor impartial. I had seen what he did in the police corruption case when he did everything he could from the bench to help the prosecution in their case against Malik Khaalis. By this ruling, it was abundantly clear to me that Judge Walmsley would go to the same lengths and greater in helping the prosecution put me away.

I was anxious to get to trial. It may sound funny, but after spending two years and seven months in limbo awaiting trial I had a comforting feeling that it would all be over soon, win, lose or draw. But because the stakes were so high, I still carried what seemed like the weight of the Earth on my shoulders.

My biggest concern was having to go up against Christy Barker, who had prosecuted the Jennifer Ross Murder and was one of the most skilled prosecutors I have ever seen in a courtroom. But I had watched her prosecution of another red ball murder of a young white girl who was beaten to death by her husband and she pulled a maneuver that warned me that she was capable of doing whatever she has to do to win a case, even lie or cheat.

Norman Smart killed his 89-pound wife by beating and stomping her so badly that the Medical Examiner was able to identify the shoes he was wearing during her autopsy. His shoe print was that recognizable on her body. It is also tragic to note that Smart had been wearing boxing gloves when he beat his wife to death.

Chris Ross was lead detective in the case. As a matter of fact, we had worked the beginning of this case together. Ross was a good guy and a good detective. He left no stone in this case unturned. Ross traveled in order to track down ex-wives and girlfriends and children who had all suffered beatings at the hands of Norman Smart. The evidence was overwhelming but a prosecutor can never be over-prepared when it comes to trial. One never knows how things are going to go once the gavel falls.

But instead of presenting all of these vivid facts exactly as they were and let them speak volumes for themselves, Ms. Barker decided to strengthen her case by playing a recorded conversation between Smart and a friend while in jail. In that call the jury heard Smart tell his friend quite urgently that he needed him to sell his boxing gloves. Ms. Barker stopped the recording and then told the jury this was Smart clearly trying to get rid of the evidence.

237

Smart's defense attorney, a cantankerous old badger named Richard Darden, objected on the grounds that the jury had not heard the rest of the recorded conversation, in which his client goes on to say to his friend, *Sell my gloves, I need money to pay my lawyer.* Smart had said nothing about getting rid of evidence, only that he needed money for his defense, and a nearly impossible one, at that.

No question Norman Smart killed his wife. Even Darden's objection to Barker's clearly intentional omission of fact and exculpatory evidence could not overcome the conviction. The fact that stands out, though, is the audacity of this officer of the Court who intentionally tried to mislead a jury on the facts of a solid case which needed no bolstering.

If Christy Barker was capable of such shenanigans in front of a jury and a Superior Court Judge, it begs the question what might she be capable of in front of a Grand Jury while seeking an indictment when there is no one there to object or point out similar omissions?

That should tell anyone all they need to know about Christy Barker.

And that did not bode well for Kevin Grogan.

I had a hard time wrapping my mind around the fact that after spending the majority of my adult life and entire professional career devoted to public service that there was a distinct possibility that I could lose my right to vote, my right to serve on a jury, and even my right to carry a gun if I were convicted. I had a real issue with that. I never had a problem with accepting responsibility for my actions but to be punished at that level for something that I did not do made me sick.

The events leading up to the trial were extremely stressful and my stomach was in a constant knot. I tried to stay busy to keep my mind occupied by other matters. The irony is that I never slept better. For the past dozen years sleep had always been difficult owing to my hectic schedule but the closer I came to trial date the problem disappeared. Meals were difficult to enjoy but when my head hit the pillow I closed my eyes and went to sleep. Each morning I would wake up feeling rested and ready to roll.

The guilty flee while the righteous stand bold as a lion. So says my favorite Proverb from the Bible. And that is exactly how I felt every morning upon arising, bold as a lion. I could not imagine a jury convicting me of lying after I had told investigators every possible truthful thing I could think of during my interviews.

I knew I was right even though the DA had charged me for all the wrong reasons.

I knew I had the best attorney in Savannah.

I knew I had the support and respect of the people I respected most.

I slept like a lion.

Chapter Sixteen
My Cousin Mikey

The first day of my trial was February 22, 2017. It was a surreal moment to be walking into the same courtroom I had appeared in as a witness for the prosecution hundreds of times and past the table where I sat next to the Assistant District Attorney and take a seat next to Mike Schiavone at the defense table instead.

Never in a million years would I have thought that I would be sitting here in this position, especially under such ridiculous circumstances.

I had known Mike for many years, had argued cases against his clients, and seen him at work. I had every confidence in my legal representation but was still having a hard time moving past the absurdity of the situation and how a simple case of driving under the influence had become a glaring example of police corruption.

There's something wrong somewhere.

My trial began as they do: the Judge explained how he wanted to see the case proceed and Ms. Barker advised the Court that I had been offered a plea to reckless driving that I had refused and went on to say that I had also been offered some sort of veteran's deferment and which I denied through my attorney.

None of this was true. But here she was, Christy Barker standing in open court, telling the Judge complete falsehoods. The DA's office had lied from the start. Why should they stop now?

All respect that I had accumulated for Barker through the years of appearing as a witness for the prosecution vanished at this point. All that remained in me was an unadulterated hatred flowing through my veins as I listened to her misrepresent the facts and enter it on the record.

Jury selection was the next order of business. Fifty people are brought in and both sides fish the pool for those who appear sympathetic to their position. It is a singularly important part of a trial but something I had never paid much attention to because I have appeared before hundreds of juries and they were all the same to me. But with over 35 years of trial experience, Mike Schiavone is an expert at Voir Dire. Now I am a detective and if it's one thing I know how to do it's read people. But Mike doesn't need any help and I had virtually little input in the jury selection process.

There was a bright moment during Voir Dire that was an omen of things to come: One of the potential jurors was a Georgia State Corrections Lieutenant in full uniform who was P.O.S.T. certified. There are rules governing such officers serving on juries. If they have arrest powers, they may not serve on a jury. ADA Barker wasted no time striking the lieutenant on the grounds that he was P.O.S.T. certified but the Judge ruled against her because the lieutenant did not have arrest powers.

I tapped Mike on the arm. *Well, I whispered, at least he ruled in our favor once!*

I got a big kick out of this minor victory but it did not last long. Judge Walmsley ruled that the doctor's report and testimony would be disallowed because the prosecution had not been notified in a timely manner. The Judge allowed Karl Knoche to testify, even though Karl's information was turned over at the same time as Dr. Odom's.

I guess the Judge figured that the United States Attorney's Office might wonder why he denied their assistant U.S. attorney's testimony.

The point that will continue to resonate within me for the rest of my days, however, is that Judge Walmsley denied the admission of commendations that I had been awarded in the army and by the police department. The reasoning he provided was that commendations did not speak to my truthfulness.

I had a sharp pain in my neck at the thought that the Judge who held my fate in his hands had no concept of what the word honor means. To me, Integrity is one of the elements of honor. While I have never claimed to be a perfect man, I am, however, an honorable man.

The rest of jury selection went smoothly and quickly and I was pleased with Mike's selection. The jury of 12, with 2 alternates, was made up of a cross section of Savannah society: male and female, black and white; they looked like every other jury I had ever appeared before.

Opening arguments went according to what I expected: Barker called me a liar and Schiavone told the truth. I was hoping Mike would go with that famous line from the movie, My Cousin Vinny, when a criminal defense lawyer played by Joe Pesci responds to the DA's opening statement, saying: Everything he just said is bullshit. But, of course, Mike was more eloquent than that.

One of the most humbling experiences in my entire life was having to sit through the opening and closing arguments of this trial. Even though I knew what the ADA was going to say, it did not ease the impact when Barker actually said it.

It was a different experience altogether watching Mike Schiavone discredit each and every witness for the prosecution. All I could hope was that the jury was seeing what I was seeing. Nothing that was presented as evidence added up to the charge of tampering nor did it constitute making false statements. Even so, I worried that I possessed a far greater understanding of what had transpired over the past two years and seven months than the jury that had no idea what really happened.

All I know is Mike Schiavone did a masterful job on cross-examination and by the time Barker rested, I was confident that she had failed to prove her case against me.

We had an altogether simple strategy: Call Karl Knoche to the stand and have him tell the jury that in his estimable opinion I am a most trustworthy individual and then I was going to take the stand and prove it.

I got my chance and Mr. Schiavone led me down an easy path. He asked me to relate my story to the jury and I did. I told them exactly what I did and did not do. I told them about the DUI and its aftermath. I told them that I had been called a liar by the same people who subpoenaed me to testify for them. I made a point of looking every member of the jury in the eyes and I told the truth.

What I saw as I testified was the nod of juror's heads and looks of sympathetic understanding. I felt like they were on my side but because the consequences were so dire, I really didn't know what to think of the jury's disposition.

243

There were no surprises at trial until the end of Barker's cross-examination of me. I stated previously that I had only seen one prosecutor better prepared than Christy Barker-- and he was my character witness-- but her weaknesses surfaced as the trial turned in my favor. Barker's fundamental flaw is the inability to adjust when things don't go her way, to wit: Barker made a tremendous mistake when she asked me about refusing to testify in the Rashaad Spann case where I plead the Fifth Amendment and the DA's office allowed a cold blooded murderer to plea to a much lesser offense.

I answered emphatically that I had never refused to testify in any case, ever. We argued back and forth about what constitutes a refusal to testify but in the end Barker made one of the worst errors I have ever seen in a courtroom, and it only got worse for the prosecution from there.

Barker called Matt Breeden to rebut my testimony about refusing to testify as a prosecution witness. Breeden was present during the Rodderick Jackson trial and argued in the 611 hearing that the Fifth Amendment did not apply to me because I was a material witness, a matter that was resolved by Chief Superior Court Judge Michael Karpf, who ruled that the Fifth did, in fact, apply. Breeden testified that I was a material witness in the Anthony Parish trial, a murder case that I had absolutely nothing whatsoever to do with.

I leaned into Mike and told him that Breeden was dead wrong and that he was probably referring to the Rashad Spann case in which Fashaad Kennedy was the suspect. Parish, Fashaad, Rashad, whomever, they were probably all the same to Breeden.

244

But Breeden was on a roll and stated that he was there when Jerry Rothschild offered a written immunity to James Byrne and I that I not only turned down but that I also refused to testify. This was factually incorrect and a direct contradiction of what Barker had asked me on cross when she accused me of refusing to testify because I was NOT offered immunity in that case.

But Breeden still wasn't done fucking up the prosecution's case when he testified that as a result of my refusing to testify that "a murderer walked out of the courtroom a free man".

I came perilously close to losing my composure because nothing Breeden could have invented was further from the truth of that last statement: neither Anthony Parish nor Fashaad Kennedy walked out of the courtroom free men.

But here's the kicker: Both Anthony Parish and Fashaad Kennedy had been tried before Judge Walmsley. Certainly the Judge was aware that neither defendant walked out of his courtroom because he sentenced them to prison. But the Judge said nothing and it appeared that the district attorney's office would stop at nothing to convict me of their heinous politically motivated charges.

At that moment, however, when Breeden testified that I let a murderer go free rather than testify, I sat by helplessly as Judge Walmsley allowed Breeden's testimony to stand. I grabbed Schiavone by the arm and told him Breeden had lied. It was the only time Mike appeared to be uneasy during the entire proceeding.

It was left to James Byrne to take the stand in my defense and rebut Breeden's testimony by explaining to the jury that I had not, in fact, been offered immunity and that I had not refused to testify but followed his advice in pleading the Fifth. He finished by assuring the jury that no murderer ever walked out of any courtroom because I had failed to testify in their hearing.

During a recess I made my way to the men's room and saw Matt Breeden waiting on the elevator. I felt a rush of adrenaline overcome me and that old fight or flight feeling kick in. It took every ounce of restraint and professional composure not to explode him in place like a land mine, as we used to say in the Army. So as I passed him by I said, *Fuck you, dude* and kept moving so that he could not spin it to have been said in a threatening manner. Breeden's reaction was exactly what I expected: he walked around in agitated circles, shaking slightly, then turned and walked as fast as he could into the courtroom where I assume he ran and told Christy that I was mean to him.

Court was adjourned but before going home I went to the Clerk's office and requested a certified copy of both Parish's and Kennedy's conviction documents in order to prove that what Breeden testified to was false. Further, it is my contention that Breeden's testimony was knowingly false. In essence, Barker had put up a witness for the State who intentionally perjured himself in order to convict me of their trumped up charges.

The next morning Mike Schiavone met privately with Judge Walmsley in chambers and informed him of Breeden's perjured testimony. According to my lawyer, the Judge showed little concern for the matter and said that it was an issue that he was not going to address.

The Judge's informal ruling did not deter Mike Schiavone from filing a more formal motion for a mistrial stating prosecutorial misconduct, asking that Breeden's entire testimony be stricken from the record. In the event the Court ruled against the motion, Schiavone wanted a continuance in order to prove Breeden's testimony was false.

Denied.

The Judge moved immediately into preparing the charging documents to enable the jury to make a decision and reach a verdict. Once the charging documents were in place, the Judge declared a recess.

I don't know exactly what happened to cause a 10-minute recess to drag on interminably but at one point Christy Barker came back in and said that the Judge had gone upstairs and by that I assumed that he was conferring with a colleague. Upon his return, Judge Walmsley granted a continuance until the following Monday, a period of three days. Schiavone put in a rush order with the court reporter for a transcription of the Breeden testimony, then worked through the weekend in putting together a motion for Mistrial.

After going over Breeden's testimony, Schiavone said there was no way to mistake that Breeden was intentionally lying. It was obvious that the district attorney's office was so crooked and hell bent on their political agenda that they lied on the stand in order to prosecute a DUI dressed up as police corruption.

Thus, the district attorney was fighting what was perceived as corruption with actual corruption; all corruption is equal. There is no difference between politics and gangsterism. Ironic, but it made me feel

247

important that the district attorney's office went to such horrible lengths in furthering their political agenda by setting aside the rules.

Mr. Schiavone's motion called for a mistrial based on the professional misconduct of both Breeden and Barker for presenting false testimony. The motion also called for Judge Walmsley to recuse himself from the case because he was a material witness in both the Parish and Kennedy cases, and Mr. Schiavone would have to call him as a witness. Mr. Schiavone also moved to make Jerry Rothschild a material witness to show that there was never any written immunity deal or any other immunity offered, and that neither Parish or Kennedy walked away from court as free men.

It took balls for Mike Schiavone to make this motion and go after the Judge in this manner. This wasn't the first time he and Judge Walmsley had mistrial issues, as recently as the Malik Khaalis case.

As expected, Judge Walmsley denied the motion for mistrial but he did reopen the evidence. Breeden was recalled to the witness stand and walked back the name Parish and acted if it was no big deal. He also conceded that no murderer walked out of any courtroom due to my having refused to testify against them. But he held onto the party line that he had worked with Jerry Rothschild on the immunity deal and that he was party to conversations held with James Byrne and I on the subject.

It was another lie and easy to prove: Had I been granted immunity, I would have testified and Kennedy would have been convicted of murder. But the DA was dug in so deep by this point they couldn't back off and do the right thing. They kept going, essentially choosing to prosecute a cop for a DUI than a cold-blooded killer for Murder.

Jerry Rothschild took the stand and testified to the fact that no immunity was offered me in the Kennedy case. I knew Jerry would not lie on the stand for anybody. I did not envy his position: he tried to clean up the mess Breeden had made and at the same time stuck to the truth that crippled the case cobbled together by his office. Jerry did reiterate that my "refusing to testify" basically "gutted" his case and was the reason why the State had to plead it down.

If the DA's office had just let me plead to the actual case and let go of their trumped up political agenda, I could have testified and justice would have been served.

I was certain that all of these lies presented to the jury must have been confusing, to say the least. By the time they took the case into deliberation, I wasn't sure who they were going to believe. The Judge certainly wasn't on my side; all fairness and impartiality were gone. Surely, the jury noticed it and were left to wonder why.

As the trial came to a close I remember coming to a realization that will stick with me for the rest of my life: I am a white American of Irish descent with an upper-middle class upbringing. I was college educated and a combat veteran who served in the United States Army. I was a decorated police officer who served with distinction. And had helped the district attorney's office win hundreds of criminal cases. But I had been sitting in the hot seat for four days and was not getting a fair trial.

And if all this could happen to me, what possible chance does a black kid from Hitch Village have at a fair trial? Or a poor white girl from Ogeechee Road?

None. They have no chance.

Chapter Seventeen
Keepin It Real

Sitting through the closing arguments presented in my trial was one of the most humbling experiences of my life.

Mike Schiavone went first and Christy Barker had the last word. Once Iron Mike was finished with his closing that was all he could do and the rest was up to the jury.

Listening to an assistant district attorney call me a liar for the better part of an hour and beam PowerPoint slides illustrating every mistake, word or gesture forced me to take a good hard look at myself. My only hope was that the jury still remembered what Mike had said in my defense after listening to Christy for an hour.

Three quarters of the way into her closing statement, Christy tried to get cute while attempting to explain circumstantial evidence. She suddenly changed her tone, became animated, and took the jury to school on that which does not have to be seen but can be inferred from the information provided. She went so far as to use the example of the child who is told not to eat chocolate cookies and of parents leaving the room and coming back to discover the child's face and hands covered in chocolate, the cookies missing from the plate. Even though the parents did not see the child eat the cookies, she said, the circumstantial evidence was all over the child's hands and face.

Then the assistant district attorney of Chatham County pointed to me and said:

He has chocolate all over him.

Had the jury laughed it might've spelled trouble. I scanned their faces and not one of them so much as cracked a smile at her attempt at humor. I found comfort in what was otherwise a woefully uncomfortable predicament.

Closing arguments concluded, the Judge went over the charging documents with the jury and explained the points of law. And then I watched the 14 men and women who were to decide my fate stand up and walk out of the courtroom. I got no indication from any single juror as to how they might be feeling at this moment. I had certainly heard enough. I hoped they had not heard too much of the wrong thing.

It is what it is, Mike said to me, *and it is in the jury's hands*. He was neither comforting nor disparaging as we walked around waiting on the verdict. It wasn't too long before a deputy notified us that the jury had a few questions. After reconvening, the jury admitted they were confused as to which false statement I was charged with making. Obviously, they had gotten lost somewhere during Barker's hour-long tirade and missed the whole point of her prosecution.

The next two questions had to do with Garrity (the advisement of rights administered by investigators to employees who are the subject of an internal investigation) and the form I signed in the administrative interview that stated nothing I said could be used against me criminally. The very fact that the jury asked about this gave me a jolt of positive reinforcement because Schiavone had said in his closing that if the jury remembered nothing else, that they should look at this form and apply the law as they see fit. And the fact that the jury was doing exactly what Mike had asked meant that the smoke and mirror PowerPoint that Christy had tried to pawn off had not clouded their vision.

The Judge provided the answers to the jury's questions and sent them back into deliberation.

The clock said the jury had been out for about an hour that seemed more like an eternity to me. I made an attempt at small talk with my lawyer, pointing out that I felt good that the jury remembered what he said and that their questions about Garrity meant that they had listened to him. Another hour passed and then the Deputy announced that the jury had reached a verdict.

No matter how good I felt about the case I did not want to be in the position I was in at this very moment. I walked slowly and deliberately into the courtroom and sat on what I've always considered to be the wrong side and watched again as these 14 individuals filed back into the jury box.

I was told to stand while the jury read the verdict. My body was tense and I was stiff in ways that would make an honor guard envious.

On count one of the false statements, the foreman said, *we the jury find the defendant not guilty.*

Mike Schiavone grabbed my right forearm with his left hand as my legs went numb. Yes, the jury had heard the evidence and had seen through the deception of what the district attorney's office had tried to do.

I will let the reader in on a little secret: For every day of the trial I kept in my pocket a challenge coin, an old military custom, but this one had been created by Toby Taylor and I for the SARGE Operation, a 2 1/2-inch antique silver finished coin with our Unit's logo and an outline of the Talmadge Bridge, and with ATF and SCMPD badges, and a Georgia and Irish flag. I kept it with me for good luck; I guess I'm more superstitious than I thought.

As the jury foreman was reading the verdict I held the challenge coin in my left hand and thought that if this doesn't go my way, I don't want to lose this coin. I started to remove the coin from my pocket and reach for my wallet. I was going to tuck the coin in a credit card fold and if they found me guilty I could, in one motion, hand off my wallet and coin and keys and phone to Mike for safekeeping. And then I thought if I take out this coin and put it in my wallet I'm giving up. I'd be resigning myself to the fact that I've lost. But after two years and seven months of fighting there was no way I could give up. So I held that coin in the tightest grip I possibly could as the verdict was read.

I was found guilty of the DUI charge, which I had conceded. Then when the tampering with evidence charge was read, I thought *there's still more bullshit out there, let's see.*

Count three, tampering with evidence, the foreman said, *we the jury find the defendant not guilty.*

The rest of my body went numb. My entire being tingled like when your foot falls asleep. I looked at the jury to find several of them smiling at me, a subtle thumbs up. I put my right hand over my heart and mouthed the words "thank you" repeatedly.

The nightmare was over.

254

Mike Schiavone had done what no other lawyer had done thus far in defending a client against a political purge devised by a misguided district attorney's office and won. I looked across to the other side and saw the assistant district attorney was flustered. Judge Walmsley asked both sides if there would be any word on sentencing.

Christy did not know what to say. Her lower lip was protruding and both hands were visibly shaking. So stunned was she by the verdict that she asked the Judge for a postponement in order to prepare something. She couldn't even stand to address the Court.

I knew from early on in this prosecution that this case was politically motivated and had nothing to do with the pursuit of justice. Barker's inability to provide the Court with an argument for a first offense DUI sentencing showed me all I needed to know about her character and motivation. Prosecutors are supposed to be fair, they're supposed to serve the community, and they swear an oath to prosecute cases in the interest of justice. Barker's reaction to the verdict showed that her prosecution of me was personal, not professional. There can be no other explanation for her actions.

At the sentencing hearing two weeks later, I got what I consider to be a typical sentence for a first-time DUI: one year probated, two days in jail, credit for time served, fines, and DUI and Alcohol classes.

Your Honor, it's obvious that throughout this case there has been a lot of posturing by both sides, Barker said, which summed up exactly what I had known and been thinking the entire time: the entire case against me was pure exaggeration, blown completely out of proportion.

When those words escaped her lips I almost shouted, I object! The only posturing from my side was a defensive one to fend off the ruthless attack from the district attorney's office. But the fact that Barker had the gall to admit that her actions during this prosecution were "posturing" made me sick to my stomach but proved everything I have said throughout this book.

*   *   *   *   *

If you ever find yourself in Savannah around lunchtime and craves the best ribs in this world, treat yourself to a trip to Randy's BBQ at the end of where Hitch Village used to stand. Go early, the line starts forming around 10:30 a.m. and if you're not there before noon, chances are you have already missed out.

I was standing in line one day recently, minding my own business and salivating from the smoke blowing from the shack when I felt a presence behind me. I turned and saw a group of guys, one of whom was none other than Hot Boy Roy. A funny feeling swept over me. I was apprehensive but at the same time kind of glad to see him. We made eye contact and it took him a few seconds but out came the wide smile and we hugged like long lost brothers.

In a matter of minutes we caught up and even got around to asking about each other's families. He was a proud new father and he wanted me to meet his new boss, who was also waiting in line for ribs.

I told Hot Boy Roy's boss that he had a fine young man working for him and the boss wanted me to know that HBR was doing well. Except that neither of us called him by his old street name and I deliberately omit

256

his given name here out of respect. I mean, it felt so good to see this young man doing well in the legit world after all the fits he gave me back in the day, chasing him around Hitch Village.

He seemed genuinely happy to see me, too, and wasn't shy about greeting me in public. Then I flashed back to the week prior, when I was in the courthouse and the number of assistant district attorneys who turned away as I walked down the hall, the ones who noticeably stopped in their tracks and changed direction as I approached in order to avoid me.

At one point I was a player on their team. I brought cases that mattered to them to finish prosecution. Cases that mattered to the community and now, because I no longer mattered to the district attorney, except to showcase how fair they are by prosecuting black sheep white cops, they could not bring themselves to look me in the eye.

Real is real, as we say on the streets of Savannah. Few people employed by the District Attorney's Office in Chatham County, Georgia are real.

Hot Boy Roy still keeps it real.

And so does Kevin Grogan

ACKNOWLEDGEMENTS

While telling this story and acknowledging great officers and people with whom I have served had been a relatively easy task.....Thank everyone who has made it happen and contributed in any way is a much more daunting task.....Here is my best effort:

To the Tytan crew, thanks for making the image that I had in my head come to life, Leah, Jim, Jim and Miss Roxey especially. Ilse and Seaward for helping me fine tune the whole thing.

I want to thank guys who are SPD and police legends, some who I could fit in the story and some who I didn't have the direct contact with but respect them from a far, guys like SGT Hucks, SGT Nichols, SGT Carroll, LT. Lee, Lt. (Chief) Glemboski, SGT "Action" Jackson, LT Manz, SGT Kijuawa, SGT Cortez, SGT Rich, MAJ (Director) Regan, CPT (Chief) Merriman, LT Stevens, SGT Elleby, SCPL Hollis, CPL Daryl Cone, APO Tony Edwards, CPL Gene Johnson, Det James "Rev" Williams, SCPL Fred Praylo, SCPL Brian Gerber, APO Shawn Kinzer, APO Warren Pippen, Bill Buttersworth, Geoff Rhors (USMS), Tommy Long (USMS), LT Flood, LT Regan, CMP3, SGT Lawhorn, SGT Mcphearson, SGT Sauer, AUSA Jenna Solari, AUSA Shayne Mayes, AUSA Cameron Ippolito, LT (Major)Wilkins, LT Wilson (who came up with the name EXPO), S/A (SAC) George Belsky and Sheriff Wilcher who continues to reaffirm my belief that anything can be accomplished if you are willing to pour your soul into it.

Ralf Bicknese, Lou Valoze and Toby Taylor, my brothers, I couldn't have made it through all of this shit without you. Loyalty, a dying art and y'all are a dying breed.

James Byrne, Don Montgomery, Steve Scheer and Mike Schiavone, you showed me the other side and opened my eyes. I can never repay the debt I have to all of you.

Trev, I'll get it all together one of these days. I'm proud of who you have become and continue to be.

J Reyna, Steve Fennel, Mike Gardner, George French, Barrett Fisher, John Cummins, Brandon Hunt, Chris Mauer, Roland Ellis, Mike Salois, Shannon and Mike Petrakos, Tom Taburski, Andrew Swilling, David Wolfe, Jethro Coe, CPT Poole and 1SG Barnes and my Enforcer family.

Mike Le, thanks for keeping me afloat....

Mom, Scan, Rook and Kelly, you all knew I was going hit the spotlight somehow, sorry it was like this but I couldn't have made it without you.

Mr. Murray Silver Jr. without you this book would never have been written. You are a master of your craft and a true friend.

My EXPO brothers.........I only have the words I have written on these pages.

Ilse...I don't know what else to say other than here it is.....

Made in the USA
Middletown, DE
27 February 2018